THE LOG OF
EL JAY

THE LOG OF EL JAY

The Voyage Home

A TRUE STORY
BY LLOYD DAVENPORT

Affiliated Writers of America
Casa Grande, Arizona

Published by Affiliated Writers of America
An Imprint of Alexander & Hayes Publishing, Inc.
P.O. Box 11107
Casa Grande, Arizona 85130
520-709-6658

Cover Art, Cover Illustration(s), and Cover Design Copyright 2010 by Alexander & Hayes Publishing, Inc.
Cover Design, Book Design, Typesetting, and Computer Graphics by Jayme Fraser

Library of Congress Control Number: 2010917136

ISBN: 978-1-879915-24-4

Manufactured in the United States of America

*To all sailors around the world
and all dreamers who dream of sailing*

CONTENTS

PART TWO

FOREWORD

When I first met Lloyd Davenport, and even as I got to know him for some nine months afterward, I had no idea that this quiet, unassuming man had been on such a journey as this, or that he had the extraordinary talent and tenacity to write this story with the intent to self-publish it. This book is yet another dream of his, which he has fulfilled. As you can see, this is not a self-published book, au contraire, it is a story which struck me as a metaphor for life and deserved publication by a national press. It is the first book he has written, and it is the twenty-third book that I have published.

It was January, 2010, when he walked into the auditorium where I taught an evening course on book publishing at Central Arizona College — a new course which I created to enable writers to understand how the industry works — and also to help them sharpen their perspectives on how to write or edit a manuscript for publication. From that day on, he wrote constantly and engaged himself in the class. His comments and questions reflected a rare ability to not only see people for what they were, but to see *into* people.

My teaching style is storytelling, and I have a gazillion stories to tell from my past, and as I shared many of these with the class, the students got to know not only the material I was presenting, but me as a person, publisher, and professor. One evening, as I was telling a story, Davenport asked me, "Do you have any regrets about switching your career from a writer to a publisher?" It was one of the most profound questions that I had ever been asked in my life. I had never really thought of it that way, and the answer was not an easy one. I struggled with the answer which ultimately led me to say something like this to the class: "When I think about what I've achieved and the life I've lived as a publisher, I wouldn't trade that for anything. So I guess my answer is no. But the question certainly makes me wonder." Although I offered an answer, I still think about that question every day. And I realized that the question had not been designed to put me on the spot in front of the class, but to enable me to understand myself and my own life in a better way. It suggested that there had been a sacrifice, a cost associated with that decision. Perhaps there had been. How could anyone know the outcome, had I stayed on the other path? When someone saw that deeply into my life, it meant something. Part of what I teach about becoming a writer is to learn to see into other people as a writer — and Davenport certainly has the gift.

Davenport was on a quest and took his seat religiously every Wednesday evening. I discovered later that he was writing not only this book — but three. When the course was over and summer upon us all, Davenport was the first to enroll in the second class I teach on book publishing — the follow-up workshop in which students actually do what they had learned to do in the first course.

When I read the manuscript for this book, which he presented to the class, I was amazed. I found myself thinking about him, seeing him in this story and on the *El Jay*, and realizing that the man in my class had lived his life in such a way that his story had something to offer all of us. I saw in this humble man a sense of courage, compassion, and a will to succeed. I saw a man with compassion even for the men who cheated him. That doesn't come easy, and as the story shows us, Davenport succeeds, but with a cautionary caveat: "Life has a way of putting dreams into perspective."

So now, Davenport fulfills yet another of his dreams—this book—and it is with great joy that I fulfill one of my own. This book will always be very special to me because it embodies the spirit of one of my dreams—that I could help someone write their book and either publish it themselves or get it published by teaching classes on how to do it. Thank you, Mr. Davenport.

This book is the first of many more to come, and I believe that anyone who reads it will find themselves on an adventure extraordinaire.

——Jay Fraser, Publisher

PREFACE

My name is Lloyd R. Davenport, and my wife's name is Judy A. Davenport. I am presently seventy-two years of age. For years, I have been telling stories to my children and grandchildren about my adventures. They insisted that I should write books about my travels. One of the most eventful tales was about a voyage in my CSY 44 sailboat. I traveled from Tortola, in the British Virgin Islands (B.V.I.), to Olympia, Washington. This voyage was spread out over two trips. The first trip entailed getting the boat ready and sailing it to the Panama Canal. The second trip was from the Panama Canal to Olympia, Washington. The two trips were completely different, but still amazingly exciting. Both of the trips were started at the beginning of hurricane season. This set things in motion that created some hair-raising adventures.

That was the time of General Noriega and the rampant drug smuggling operations in Panama. The year was 1985, and it was common knowledge on the street that Noriega was involved. Just prior to Noriega taking over the government, there was a rumor that the leader of Panama was in a mysterious helicopter explosion with his second-in-command. Both men were killed, and Noriega took over the reins of leadership. It was generally assumed that Noriega and the drug dealers were behind it. The United States government was cracking down on drug smuggling from Panama, and our relationship with Panama was strained because of it.

There was another rumor about the anchorage offshore at Cristobel, Panama. It was said that if you wanted a weapon, you only had to go scuba diving on the anchorage (The Flats). Boats approaching the Panama Canal from the east would throw their weapons over the stern to keep from being caught with weapons on board. Just before leaving, on the Pacific side, they would purchase new weapons on the black market.

ACKNOWLEDGMENTS

I would like to recognize Professor Jay Fraser for his forethought in providing an opportunity for me to realize the culmination of a dream. That dream was to create a record of one of my sailing trips. An article about the Fundamentals of Book Publishing course appeared in the *Casa Grande Dispatch*. The *Dispatch* is a wonderful newspaper, and the article caught my eye. On an impulse, I signed up for the class.

I would also like to thank Professor Jay Fraser for creating the two courses in book publishing and teaching them — the second course being a workshop. Both classes were taught one evening a week. Professor Fraser provided me with the skills and encouragement to put my dream down on paper and be published. It was through his efforts at Central Arizona College and all of the other people involved in the total program that my book has come alive. My book is only the first of many to come from the workshop, and I am hopeful that the leaders of Central Arizona College will not allow my one small step to be the last. I can only hope that my publication will be an inspiration for all who seek to fulfill their dreams in the coming years. You must follow your path of life.

Professor Fraser has been a beacon of light to follow during the many long hours that I have had to spend researching this book. He has never tired of my many questions and never faltered with his answers. Without his guidance, this book would never have been written. He and his daughter, Jayme Fraser, whom I would also like to thank, were my teachers in the various nuances that are necessary in compiling a book by a novice such as myself, and the computer is becoming my friend. Besides being my professor, he has been my mentor, my publisher, and my friend. Every day spent in his class was a wonderful, enlightening experience. To each and everyone at Central Arizona College that provided assistance to Professor Fraser for his program, I would like to thank you from the bottom of my heart. You must know that being in my book puts you forever in my thoughts.

I must also thank my lovely wife Judy for her infinite patience and wisdom. I have struggled with this book many times during these past years, and she was always there for me. My four children, Wayne Pifer, Tom Pifer, Linda Schmitt (Davenport), and Loren Davenport, were my inspiration. They kept asking me when I was going to write about the stories that I had been telling them for years. I thank them all for their persistence.

PART ONE

CHAPTER ONE
The Voyage Begins

The wind was howling, and it threatened to blow the *El Jay* over onto its starboard side. I grabbed the sheet (rope) off of the starboard self-tailing winch, and it flew through my fingers. The flesh on my fingers was torn and burned from the rope. This relieved the pressure on the jib. The jib was now flapping in the wind, but the threat to the boat from the other two sails was still there. We lowered and reefed the main and dropped the staysail to the deck. With the engine racing, we slowly maneuvered the bow of the boat into the wind. The wind was tearing at the jib that was still flapping wildly in front of the boat. We pulled hard and were finally able to rewind the jib onto the roller furling. We steered into the very large waves breaking across our bow and tried to ride out this sudden storm. Except for the injuries to my bleeding fingers and hands, nobody else was hurt or killed on that day, but I felt that it was close at times. Let me start at the beginning.

My wife Judy and I had purchased a 1978 CSY 44 sailboat from CSY Yacht Corp. The yacht had been in charter from January of 1978 through April of 1985. It was a cutter-rigged yacht with a main, staysail, and roller-furling jib. I had enlisted the aid of many friends and acquaintances to help me bring the boat home to Olympia, Washington. Bill Brandt and his wife Jodie traveled with Judy and me to the Island of Tortola, British Virgin Islands (BVI). The time of year was near the end of April, 1985. We were there to check on the status of the boat. The boat had been in charter with Caribbean Sailing Yachts. They were the charter arm of CSY Yacht Corp. We found the boat to be in very bad need of repair.

I had sent a young couple, Jeff and Cris Sibold from Olympia, to attend to the boat. They were to evaluate the boat for one month, make the necessary repairs, and assist me in bringing the boat home through the Panama Canal. Bill, Jodie, Judy, and I were there with many of the items needed to prepare the boat for the long voyage home. Most of these things were brought from Olympia because they were not available in the BVI. We stowed the extra gear necessary for the trip, and the six of us headed out on a shakedown cruise. We had many problems to overcome, but we felt like we were on the right track. That feeling was soon to disappear.

Just after noon, we left the CSY dock at Roadtown, Tortola, BVI and headed south. The sails were down for the short trip to the first night's anchorage. We stopped at Norman Island well before nightfall. That island had cattle that came down to the water's edge and drank the saltwater. I had seen this happen on other trips, but we did not get to see them this time. We set the anchor and enjoyed a cool gin and tonic. Life was good and this was going to be a wonderful trip. We enjoyed a quiet dinner and turned in early. The red-eye flight from Olympia to Tortola had taken its toll.

The next morning we headed east toward Marina Cay. The sails were full and the boat was flying. The winds were blowing at ten- to fifteen-miles-per-hour, and we tacked back and forth into the wind as we traveled up Sir Francis Drake Channel. Marina Cay was just offshore of the east end of Tortola. It was a small, circular island with a very protected anchorage. We arrived before 2:00 PM and watched the other boats come in and try to anchor. When you were one of the first to anchor, it was easy. If you were one of the last, and the anchorage was crowded, that could be a disaster. We watched as one of the boats motored across another boat's anchor line and severed it, and that action put the previously anchored boat adrift. It was not pretty, but our rum and cokes were nice as we watched the action.

We left the next morning and headed for Virgin Gorda Island. The sailing was great and the sun was shining. It could not get any better than that. We anchored on a buoy just off of the beach at the Bitter End Resort. That resort and the adjoining resort at Biros Cove were very beautiful. From the Biros Cove Resort, you could see out across the Atlantic Ocean. Once you headed east from Virgin Gorda, there was nothing but water until you reach the African Coast. Looking west, you could look down on all of the boats anchored in the bay. There was another area called the Baths, and it was outstanding. Large boulders formed shallow pools for snorkeling and swimming. These three locations are a must-see if you ever get to the Virgin Islands.

The next morning we set sail and headed north to Anegada Island. Prior to our arrival, we had radioed ahead and ordered dinner. The sun was overhead and we could see all of the large coral heads hidden just below the surface of the water. They were waiting for a careless boater. We had a great sail and anchored just after 2:00 PM. for the night. We had a wonderful lobster dinner. The lobster was cooked in a fifty-five-gallon drum that had been split in half from top to bottom. They killed live lobsters and then cut them in half. They wrapped them with aluminum foil and made a lobster boat. The fire consisted of hot coals from local mesquite wood. They constantly basted the lobster with butter and then served it family style with vegetables. The entire meal was out of this world.

The next morning we sailed north around Anegada and then headed southeast toward St. Martin Island. We were in open water after we cleared the reef on the south end of Anegada. Anegada Island was the only reef island in the BVI that was inhabited and was forbidden territory for charter boats to travel to. The island was about eighteen-miles long, but only about twenty-five feet above sea level. By the time you saw the island, you were right on top of it. There was extremely shallow water surrounding the island, and many large, submerged shoals on the south end of the island. Many ships had gone aground and been salvaged. You had to be extremely cautious.

We were headed for St. Martin Island, and we were on a beam reach. The wind was off the stern on the port side. All of the sails were up, and the boat was sailing like a dream in the heavier seas of the open water. When we were just east of the submerged shoals on the south end of the island, disaster struck. I was at the helm and the wheel went slack. The steering cable had broken.

Suddenly, I had no control over the boat. The boat quickly spun to starboard, pushed by the prevailing winds. The reef was straight ahead. I remembered that the CSY 44 was supposed to have an emergency tiller under the mattress in the aft cabin. I raced to the aft cabin, pulled the mattress away, and was relieved to see the emergency tiller laying under the mattress. I immediately mounted the emergency tiller and opened the rear hatch. I put my head through the opening and stood there, looking forward at the crew. I was amazed at what I saw.

The young couple, Jeff and Cris, were busy pulling down the main. Jodie was taking down the staysail. Judy was pulling on the dinghy line to pull it in tight, as the dinghy had been trailing behind. Towing the dingy behind the boat was normal in all of the Virgin Islands. Bill was busy pulling in the jib on the roller furling. I looked at them and realized something. In four days, we had become a well-oiled machine. Nobody had to be told what to do. It had all become natural for us to react correctly. Bill finished with the jib and started the engine. The four-cylinder, Westerbeke diesel engine sprang to life. With me steering the boat with the emergency tiller, and Bill running the engine controls, the boat was now under control.

We were safe for the moment. We veered northward, slowly pulling away from the dangerous reef. We had been lucky this time, but we knew our luck could not hold out forever. Time was running out for us to reach the safety of landfall before dark. About halfway back to Anegada, Bill and Jeff changed places at the wheel, but I stayed at the tiller.

We headed back to Anegada Island because it was unsafe to continue without normal steering capability, hoping for a safe anchorage before the sun was too low in the sky. Arriving at Anegada after three o'clock was extremely dangerous. The sun illuminates the coral heads from ten o'clock until three o'clock. If you arrive at any other time, you risk going aground. It was already past noon, and we still had to go around the north end of Anegada Island to stay away from the large reef on the south end of the island. When we finally arrived at the west side of Anegada, it was getting dark. In the half-light, we could no longer see the coral heads below the surface. While I steered with my head stuck through the rear hatch, Jeff, at the wheel, ran the throttle to control the speed of the boat as we headed toward the shore. The other four crewmembers were forward on the bow watching for coral heads. We inched along and feared for the disaster waiting for us in the shallow water.

The CSY 44 draws six-and-one-half feet of water, and the depth-finder alarm was set for ten feet. It was screaming at us because the shallow water beneath the boat was changing depths rapidly. Each one of us held our breath and prayed we would not hit a coral head. We then had some good news and some bad news. The good news was that we didn't hit a coral head, but the bad news was that we went aground. We were at least one-hundred-yards offshore when we hit. We were traveling very slowly, and then we were not moving. Nobody felt us hit, but hit we did. It was still light enough to check the bottom of the boat, which we did, and it was not damaged. We had grounded on a sandy ledge.

The CSY 44 is an extremely heavy boat, 37,000 pounds dry weight, and we were stuck solidly. We could not back off of the ledge. We tried everything, but she would not budge. It was now dark, and we were all exhausted from the trials of the day. We decided to wait until tomorrow to proceed. We knew that in the Virgin Islands there was only one tide per day. It was normally a one-foot tide. None of us knew if we had grounded on the high or the low tide. We could have set another anchor and used the winch to pull us off, but decided it was a problem for the next day.

What we didn't know, but the locals did, was that this was the time of the spring tides. The high tide could be as much as three- to four-feet above normal. At about three o'clock in the morning, I felt the boat shift in the sand. It was a slight motion, but all of the crew had felt it. We all immediately ran for our assigned stations. We started the engine and gingerly motored the *El Jay* out of the sand. We knew that there was nothing directly behind us. We eased the boat back about twenty feet and then anchored the boat again. Now we could sleep, but in the morning we would have to motor the boat back to the CSY dock where we could get our steering fixed. We spent the next three days motoring back to Roadtown, Tortola, and we finally made it.

The Caribbean Sailing Yacht Charter Base (no longer in business) was located in Roadtown, Tortola in the British Virgin Islands. The town had a well-protected harbor and was situated in about the middle of Tortola Island. The entrance to the harbor was from the south, and the harbor was on the south side of the island. We arrived at about noon, with me at the tiller and my head through the hatch. Bill was at the wheel controlling the speed of the engine. Jeff was at the bow ready to tie us to the dock when we arrived. We pulled up to the dock, tied the boat to the docking cleats, disembarked from the boat, and then kissed the dock as if we had been blessed. This was not the typical storybook trip we had been expecting. This was real, and it could be dangerous at times. You had better bring your "A" game if you wanted to play in this league. People die out at sea all of the time, and nobody really knows how many or why.

The workers at Caribbean Sailing Yachts fixed the steering problem along with a dozen other small problems. The old, weather-beaten boat was as ready as it could be. But now it was time for Bill, Jodie, and Judy to leave for home. They were the smart ones, as I was soon to find out. I put them on an airplane in St. Thomas, U.S.V.I., and returned to Tortola to wait for the rest of the crew. I was so lucky to have had this amazing crew. Bill and Jodie owned a large schooner named *Suva*. They were very capable sailors. They and my wife Judy had been wonderful assets in getting the boat ready for the trip.

Gene and Margret Sibold arrived the next day to replace them as part of my new crew. They were both avid sailors, and Gene had just retired as Port Commissioner for Thurston County, Washington, which is located at the south end of Puget Sound. They were very excited to have their first offshore experience. They stowed their gear on board, and started becoming familiar with the boat. Gene and Margret were considered two of the premier sailors in the Pacific Northwest. Together, they had won just about every race they had ever entered. They sailed out of the Olympia Yacht Club in Olympia, Washington. Their son Jeff and his wife Cris had just returned from two years sailing in the South Pacific. I met them as a member of the Olympia Yacht Club, and they were all highly recommended to me. I must say, it was an honor to sail with them. That family was to be my crew on the journey to Olympia, and they made an arduous journey far less arduous.

We decided to leave the next day and head for St. Thomas for final provisioning. We were loading the final food supplies when another problem hit. Just before we untied the boat, we all decided to use the head in the main cabin one last time. It was the last time, and the worst. The head was plugged up, and we had to tear it completely apart to fix it. The insides were completely worn out and had to be replaced. We took this as an omen, and decided to have one last day in Roadtown to reflect on the trip we were about to embark upon. The weather was iffy and the hurricane season in the Caribbean was closing in fast. We would be lucky to get to the Panama Canal without some bad weather.

We went into town and had a great time. The local steel band was awesome, and the rum and cokes were strong. Tomorrow was the official start of the homeward voyage for the *El Jay*. If only I had known what was waiting for all of us.

CHAPTER 2
The Open Water

The trip to St. Thomas was slow and the heavy rainfall did not make anyone happy. We motor sailed most of the way. There was almost no wind; there was only the drenching rain running down my back.

We arrived at St. Thomas and anchored in the protected harbor just behind Water Island. We took the dingy into shore, and we each had a list. Each list had items necessary for the trip, and we set off to get them. I added one item to my list that was not on their list of things needed. It was a mosquito net, queen size, and I picked up three. When I returned to the boat they gave me quite a razzing about it. I didn't care. I had heard about the malaria bugs and wanted no part of them.

We spent another day in St. Thomas filling the fuel and water tanks. I called my wife Judy and told her that we were off. I would call when we arrived at the next stop on our journey. Everyone had high spirits and we all had plans for a comfortable trip. The weather was perfect and the wind was steady at about ten knots. We had heard of some bad weather north of us, but decided that it would not affect us. We were on a beam reach, with the wind off our stern on the port side. We were headed for Culebra Island. This was the life, and I was born to live this way.

The trip to Culebra was very smooth, Jeff was taking readings using his sextant, and we had a LORAN that gave us accurate latitude readings. The boat handled the open water like a dream and was extremely dry on deck. We anchored in the harbor at Culebra Island in what was considered the best hurricane hole in the Caribbean. We spent two nights at anchor, and it was very humid. The mosquitoes were bad, but my mosquito netting worked wonders. There were lots of mangrove plants, and that meant bugs.

We then left for the Island of Puerto Rico with a fair wind and clear skies. We motor sailed to Salinas — a safe harbor on the south side of Puerto Rico.

Just before arriving at Salinas, a very black cloud appeared out of nowhere. It was to the south of us and Jeff was at the helm. I asked him if he wanted to reduce sail, but he thought we would get a lift from it. It hit the *El Jay* broadside to port and almost knocked us down. If we had rolled over, it would have been a death sentence for us.

I also wrote about this storm at the beginning of Chapter One because it was my first bad experience out in open water, and I wanted the reader to know from the very first page what a storm at sea could do to a crew and a boat. That first burst of wind took us entirely by surprise and caught us completely off guard. It hit us so hard and so all-at-once that I thought we were dead. It was near panic with which I had grabbed the rope holding the roller-furling jib to release the rope holding the jib off the winch, and it ripped through my hands—tearing the flesh on my fingers—before I could let go. I was lucky one of my fingers or hands didn't get caught in the rope, or I would have lost a finger or been thrown overboard to drown. The middle of the sail flapped in the wind all the way to the top with no restraint along the edge to keep it tight. This was fine. At least there was no pressure on the boat now from the jib, because if I hadn't released it, the *El Jay* would have been knocked down onto its side — and sank.

Because my hands had been damaged so badly, I was not able to help the crew any further in dealing with the storm, and I went below to take care of the burns on my hands. The rest of the crew tended to saving the *El Jay*. The rain came down in buckets and it was the most intense rain I had ever been in. We had survived our first tragedy, but would we survive the next one, or the one after that? We had finally been able to roll up the jib even though the rain was intense. It had taken a beating while it was flapping around in the wind.

When the storm finally subsided, we motored on to Salinas. The entrance to the bay was very narrow with a depth of seven to ten feet. It opened into a beautiful bay with a depth of about fifteen feet. The shoreline was ringed with retirement-type houses, and the setting was like a picture that had come to life.

After anchoring, it was necessary to repair the jib. The materials on hand were limited. We used a hammer, an ice pick, and some nylon cording that I had brought along. We used a piece of wood as a table and hammered holes into the edges of the jib.

Then we fed the cord through the holes and laced them using a ladder-stitch. The stitching on the jib had been torn loose about fifteen feet on either side of the clew and would not have survived the trip to Panama. We would repair it correctly in Panama.

We left the next morning for Ponce. It was the second largest city in Puerto Rico. The Ponce Yacht Club gave us twenty-four hours of free moorage to prepare for our offshore trip to Panama. The club was beautiful, and the locals were wonderful. They helped us find everything we needed to continue on our trip to Panama.

The next morning we set off for the Panama Canal. We noticed that the air seemed to be electrically charged and the seas were a little unsettled. We tuned the ham radio to get the weather and found out that there was a tropical depression over Martinique Island. We were going to get some weather on the trip south. Because we were going offshore, and especially because of the threat of bad weather, we put the dingy on deck. It covered one of the hatches completely because of its size. It was the only place on the boat where we could put it. You have probably guessed by now that the hatch that was covered was mine. The closed hatch meant no air in that part of the cabin for the rest of the trip. I was so lucky. I had never been offshore and that did not sound good.

We set up a twenty-four-hour watch system for night watch coverage. During the day, our hours were flexible, but the hours at night were firm. My watch started at two-thirty in the morning and lasted until five. My shift overlapped that of the two women. When Cris was just going off, I went on and Margret was on shift with me for an hour-and-a-half more. Then Gene would relieve Margret and help me with my shift. I had called my wife just before we left and had told her we would be offshore for seven to ten days. I was to call her upon reaching the Panama Canal. There would be nothing but open water ahead.

The first full day went very smoothly, and we motor sailed at about six knots. That would be about 140+ miles per day. That was what we had hoped would be a normal day. Once, a U.S. Coast Guard airplane came by at eye level, and Jeff was able to contact them on the ham radio. They were very friendly as they checked us out, circled us once, and then flew away.

The next day we noticed that the wind had shifted and was coming in almost dead astern. The seas were a little more mixed and the swells were larger than the day before. We estimated them to be about fifteen-feet high. We were making good time over the water. The overcast made it impossible to take a reading with the sextant, but the LORAN still gave us a usable latitude reading. Hot food was becoming a thing of the past because of the excess motion of the boat.

The next night I had trouble sleeping. The boat was being tossed around. It was almost time for my shift at 2:30 AM, so I got up at two o'clock and went on deck. Margret was at the wheel, and the boat was flying. The sky was pitch black, and the wind was howling. She was having trouble and asked me to take the wheel. When I did, I immediately felt the stern try to break loose. The *El Jay* had a large, skeg-mounted rudder. If it broke free, the boat would swap end-for-end. I knew immediately that we had too much sail up. I asked the two women to lower some sail. They had already lowered the staysail, but they were unable to roll up the jib or lower the main by themselves. The engine was running, but it was only idling. We had no need for engine power because the boat was exceeding hull speed without it. The hull speed on the CSY

44 is 7.65 knots, and the knot meter was reading a constant 10 knots.

We had to wake Jeff and Gene to help with the sails. We could not turn the boat sideways to relieve the pressure on the sails because now the swells were twenty-feet high or higher, which would have caused us to roll over.

Both Gene and Jeff decided that to take the pressure off of the jib, they would have to reef the main under full load. That was a very scary thing to do when you were two hundred miles offshore. The boat was pitching, and it was so dark that we were working by flashlight. Gene and Jeff were up to the task, and if you had to put your life in someone's hands, find a crew like them. There was no moon and no stars, just total blackness.

They tied lines through the two reef points on the main. Those they looped around the boom. They tied off one end and had the women slowly loosen the halyard on the main. They pulled on the loose ends of the lines that had been fed through the reef points, and the extra leverage allowed them to reef the main. This relieved the tension on the roller furling, and they were able to roll up the already damaged jib.

The seas continued to build and were coming right up our stern. The scary part of it was, it was pitch black. We estimated that the seas now had grown to a height of about twenty-eight feet. We had running lights on either side of the stern, and they were turned on. With them on, I was able to see each swell as it came past the stern. The moment I saw it starting to crest, I turned the boat slightly to port and started surfing down the swell. That allowed me to quarter the trough and not bury the bow. If I had buried the bow straight into the trough, the *El Jay* would have flipped end-over-end, and we probably would have died at sea. I then turned slightly to starboard and rode the next swell back to its peak. That maneuver kept us on course.

The *El Jay*'s knot meter was still consistently reading 9.5 to 10 knots. This speed was with no engine throttle, idling only. The only sail up was a deep-reefed main. I was glad when my shift was over and I could rest. The strain on our arms was exhausting, and we switched off with one another when we got tired. It was the longest two-and-a-half hours of my life. These conditions continued for the next three days. The boat was flying and everyone was exhausted. We could not get any sextant readings because of the weather. The LORAN (land-based radio aid to navigation) was no longer of any use because we were too far from any land-based radio station, and we could not see any other boats in the area. My adrenalin was still pumping, and I was having a ball. I asked Margret if she was having fun yet, and she said she was not amused. She had expressed a sense of apprehension during the whole trip, and at this moment, she had no sense of humor.

The morning of the sixth day at sea, the storm finally ended, everything calmed down, and we could see many large ships off in the distance. The sky was still overcast, so we still had no sextant readings and thusly no navigational input from any source.

The ships directly in front of us all seemed to be heading to the west of us. Later in the morning we spotted land, and as we approached we spotted a little coastal freighter. We were able to get him to stop so we could talk to him and get directions. The other four crewmembers thought we were west of the Panama Canal and should head east, but I was convinced it was just the opposite. None of us spoke very much Spanish. I pointed east and said, "Panama Canal que?" Then I pointed west and said, "Panama Canal que?" The freighter captain smiled and pointed his finger west. He said, "Panama Canal," and off we headed, west toward the canal.

The ships to our starboard were indeed headed for the Panama Canal, and so we followed them. We headed toward the west, motor sailing, and we were glad to know that we were headed toward the Panama Canal.

It started getting late, but because we couldn't get any sextant readings, we did not know exactly where we were. So we decided to find an anchorage and rest. It had been a long, open-water passage, and we looked forward to a nice, safe anchorage. We were onshore, headed for the Panama Canal, and I had realized something. I had told my wife that we would be at sea for seven to ten days. Because of the storm conditions, we had made the trip in just six days flat.

We rounded a point of land and saw a nice place to anchor. The anchorage was behind and island we later found out was Isla Grande, a very small island. As we approached the anchorage, we noticed another boat at anchor, also. The boat was a schooner, about sixty feet in length, and made out of wood. There was a man, a woman, and a small child sitting in the cockpit of the boat. They watched us as we started to anchor and smiled when we were completed. We breathed a sigh of relief knowing we had a safe spot and set the anchor for the night. We were happy for a good night at anchor, and to sleep well for the first full night in many long days.

We had been flying in the heavy seas, and after speaking with the man on the schooner, we discovered that we had hit land very close to the canal. Because of the clouds, we had not been able to get any sextant readings for five days. We only had compass readings and dead reckoning. Jeff had been a wonder. We had hit land in Panama about forty miles east of the canal. If not for a one-knot current running along the shore from the west to the east, we would have hit the canal right on the nose.

The next morning, when we tried to leave for the canal, the engine would not start. The oil level was up, but it just would not run. Jeff and I both tried to start the engine, but it would not turn over. It was seized. Jeff rowed over to the other boat in the harbor and asked for assistance. The owner agreed to tow us to the canal. It was only hours away. When I asked him how much money he wanted to tow us, he laughed. He said, "Buy me some fuel and a couple of boxes of beer, and we'll call it square." What a wonderful person to meet in our time of need.

The vessel pulling us was a hand-built, wooden schooner named *Silva*. It had been built locally from native woods, and was about sixty feet long. The engine was a Ford, six-cylinder diesel. The CSY 44 weighs 37,000 pounds dry, and that boat pulled us through the water like we had no weight at all. It was amazing.

The skipper/owner of the schooner was Norm Bennett, an Australian. He was traveling with his wife Cindy, a Columbian. They also had their two-year-old son Pablo on board. We watched in amazement as Norm steered the boat. Little Pablo, naked as the day he was born, walked along the deck and brought him cold beer. It cooled him down in the hot sun of Panama. The little boy had absolutely no fear when it came to that big boat. Those three people were some of the nicest we were to meet on the whole trip. I think of them with the fondest of memories to this day.

The entrance to the Panama Canal is located at the city of Cristobal in the Canal Zone. It is a sister city right next to the city of Colon, just outside of the Canal Zone. The protected water inside of the jetty at the canal is called The Flats. You must anchor there to await clearance and instructions before entering

Panama and transiting the canal. We anchored at about 3:00 PM, and were cleared to travel to the Panama Canal Yacht Club for repairs at about 7:00 PM. We decided to wait until morning to travel to the yacht club.

The next morning Norm showed up early and towed us to the yacht club. We tied the stern to the dock with our bow anchored forward in the shallow water. We had showers, did laundry, and called home. Life was getting better. We had made it from Ponce in Puerto Rico to the Panama Canal in just one week.

CHAPTER 3
The Panama Canal

The **Panama Canal Yacht Club was very** secure and completely fenced. They had a security guard at the gate at all times. We were advised not to go into Colon alone, as it was not a safe place to be. The first day at the dock, a young man came up to me and asked about the boat. I told him I was the owner, and we were getting repairs. He tried to get me to carry a load of drugs up to Miami, Florida for him. I had a very hard time getting rid of him. I finally just flat out told him that he needed to move along. The unemployment in Colon was bad, and people were desperate for money.

I visited another boat to ask about any qualified mechanics, and when I left the boat my foot slipped on the dock. I was barefoot at the time, and my foot caught on the edge of the dock. I ripped the pad on the big toe of my right foot. The tear was deep and quite serious. Jeff and the yacht-club security guard, Edwin, helped me get to the clinic in town to get medical attention. It took six stitches to close the wound. Well, so much for things getting better.

By the way, did I mention that the monsoon rains were just starting? As you can see, things were not going too well. The boat engine was in need of a complete overhaul. Saltwater had seeped in through the exhaust and into the engine crankcase. This contaminated the oil with saltwater.

The boat was not wired for shore power. So the refrigerator/freezer was powered by electric current supplied by the engine when it was running. Without running the engine, we were unable to keep our food cold. We either ate it or threw it out.

I finally located a Swedish diesel mechanic to rebuild the engine. We then moved the boat up next to the yacht-club office. This allowed us to tie up to the main dock on our starboard side. We had the engine removed and taken into the chandlery at the yacht club. The engine was to be rebuilt and installed back into the boat within one week.

The engine had been taken completely apart and was in pieces within one day, and then the mechanic had to wait for the parts to be sent from CSY Yacht Corp. in Tampa, Florida. The parts were to be shipped by Eastern Airlines Sprint. That would ensure that the customs clearance would be done on the Caribbean side of Panama. Because of the way the parts were packaged, the package exceeded the weight limit for Eastern Airlines Sprint. The parts were then rerouted to Lloyds Aero Americano, ensuring that the parts would be going through customs on the Pacific side of Panama. As we struggled to get this completed, the local truckers decided to go on strike. They closed down the main, and only highway, across the isthmus. It took an additional two weeks to get the parts to the mechanic. By the time the parts showed up, the chandlery had been shut down and padlocked for back taxes. I was lucky enough to get my engine, in parts, out of there. The mechanic was now out of work, except for my engine. The parts to rebuild it had not yet been delivered and everything was on hold. Things continued to go smoothly on all fronts as you can clearly see.

During all of this, I had been actively trying to swap boats with one of the canal pilots. He had a thirty-six-foot Cheoy Lee Robb for sale. He wanted to trade up to a bigger boat and would give me a good deal. I decided to pursue this route as an alternative and hired a surveyor to check out the boat. The Cheoy Lee was a beautiful boat, and that one was a ten on a scale of one to ten. The boat was made of teak on the outer hull, but the interior was not. The survey came back negative. They had found termites in the boat. Things were not going as I had hoped, and the window for sailing up the west coast was closing. There had already been two hurricanes in the Pacific and the season had just started. I was now seriously trying to sell the boat "as is." The canal pilot who was also the owner of the Cheoy Lee started correcting the termite problem as I looked for any other alternatives. There were many other boats for sale, but none stirred my imagination.

CHAPTER 4
Unusual Experiences

*D*uring that time in Panama, unusual experiences happened to us while at the canal. When we arrived at the Panama Canal, we were required to report to the Port of Entry. The man sitting at the desk asked for our passports. All five of us gave him our passports, and then he requested money for the permits to go through the canal. I gave him the money and requested my passport back. I was informed that each of us would have to pay fifteen dollars to get them returned. When I asked for a receipt, the man pointed a hostile finger at me and shouted, "There will be no receipts for any of you!" It was good to know that graft was still alive and kicking.

About one week later in the evening, I was sitting at the bar in the yacht club. One of the pilots for the canal came in and asked for a double shot. The man was an acquaintance of mine, so I asked him if he was okay. He said he had received some bad news about the canal. The Americans had turned the maintenance of the canal over to the Panamanians. That was part of the process for turning the canal over to complete Panamanian control. The new manager, in charge of repairs for the locks, had made a bad decision. It was about the doors that open and close for each lock. The locks must be shut down one at a time to clean the accumulated trash out of each one. The locks were then inspected for damage, and were repaired as needed. The doors were very old and were part of the original locks. They were checked for damage and holes and repaired as needed. Those doors were full of air to make them light. That allowed them to be moved by a very small motor about the size of a Volkswagen engine. The makers of those doors and motors were no longer in business, and there were very few replacement parts available. That was a yearly scheduled maintenance, but the new manager said that they could not afford to shut down the locks. He said it would cost too much money for the two weeks necessary to get the maintenance done. My friend was drinking to the eventual end of the Panama Canal as he knew it. I thought about what he had said, and ordered another drink for him and one myself. I was witnessing the end of an era. That healing process continued as other people in the club also bought him drinks to help him deal with the real pain he was feeling. He had been there for over twenty years, and that was the first scheduled maintenance that had been bypassed.

CHAPTER 5
The People That You Meet

To keep myself supplied with money, it was necessary to borrow against my Visa card. To do this, I had to go into the city of Colon to one of the local banks. I would do this about once every week. I got to know the people in that department very well. That became a simple matter, except for one special trip. I had just sat down, when the front door was thrown open with a loud noise. I jumped up as if I had been shot. I turned to see what had happened and was surprised to see uniformed soldiers with M16 rifles coming in through the door. These were the Noriega years in Panama.

A woman had been helping me with my Visa card. She grabbed me and pulled me over to the wall.

We stood there with our backs to the wall as she tried to get me to be silent. Two uniformed soldiers held the door open and six more took up places around the room. When the room was deemed secured, the leader signaled to the people outside to come forward. Three men in dark suits and with briefcases entered the bank. They walked over to an office door across the room. They were invited into the room, and then the door was closed behind them. Was this drug-money laundering?

I tried to get the woman to tell me what was going on. All she would do was shake her head sideways and put her index finger vertically to her mouth. The look of fear on her face was very real, and I was sure that incident had happened before. Everyone in the bank and all visible employees stood with their backs to the walls. Banking completely stopped.

The three men came out about fifteen minutes later and exited the building. The uniformed soldiers followed them out of the building and closed the door behind them. The people in the bank went back to work as if nothing had happened. I again tried to get the woman helping me to explain, but she was too afraid. I still do not know what transpired that day, but the memories are still very clear. That was a time of transition for the canal. We were starting to turn it over to the Panamanians, and many strange things were happening.

Some of the positives that happened in Panama were the various types of people that I was able to meet. One of them was a pilot for the Panama Canal Company. His job was to help each large ship transit the canal. I was talking with him one evening about the cargo ships that were tied up to the dock directly across from the yacht club. Only three large ships could tie up at any one time. On that particular evening, there were two ships tied to the dock. I happened to ask if he knew what they were carrying, and he replied. "The ship that is first in line is carrying weapons to the Contras in Nicaragua." I was full of disbelief and told him so. He had me take a picture of the two ships and said that he would show me his pictures the next time we met. He said he had a surprise for me.

Two days later, he met me at the yacht club with his own pictures, and there was a picture of the same ship. The ship was also tied to the dock across from us. The ship was in another position on the dock with other ships around it. I was at the canal when that ship had arrived and when it had left the day before, but none of those pictures he was showing me were like mine. That ship had been through the canal before, and he had pictures to prove it. He then proceeded to tell me a story about a friend of his in law enforcement. He had boarded that ship on one of its many trips through the canal. When they looked at the containers on deck, they looked to be phony and of no use. He had checked the hold and found lots of heavy cannons and boxes. The boxes were full of what he assumed were the shells for them. They were escorted from the ship when the captain of the vessel found out that they were aboard. I was skeptical until we compared our pictures.

The top deck was loaded with containers stacked four high. The containers were of different colors. There were white ones, brown ones, and black ones. Some of them were shorter than the others, and so the stacks varied in height. The chances against those containers being stacked in the same order, and with the same white ones being placed in the same places more than once, were astronomical, but there they were. They were identical in every way and stacked in the same order.

He also said that one evening they had heard gunfire outside of the yacht club. When they ran to see what was happening, they were able to see two Russian sailors running into the jungle. The local authorities hid them there until the ship left. They had jumped overboard from the same ship as the one in my pictures, but on a different occasion. At that time, I was unsure of what he was saying. Upon further checking with other people, that incident seemed to be common knowledge.

Jeff had met some new people, and one of them agreed to help him learn another form of navigation. That involved using a calculator. The girl helping him was a wonderful young sailor, Tania Aebi. She was sailing single-handedly around the world. She was from the East Coast. It has been so many years, that I am not sure I can remember everything correctly, but I know that she wrote a book about her trip. I believe the title of the book was *Maiden Voyage*. I am sure, however, about the way we all felt about her. She was about eighteen and wonderful. She had invited me to tour the small boat she was sailing in, and I was impressed with its construction. It was very small. She was trying to get the reverse gear in the transmission on her boat repaired before transiting the canal. She spent a lot of time on the Caribbean side of Panama, so we were able to spend some time with her. She was very funny and told us many stories about her trip. I made it a point to follow her adventures in *Cruising World Magazine* and was pleased with her success. I did notice that some of the stories I was privileged to hear were not in the magazine (Tania, your secrets are safe with me).

Herme Dekiere also was very interesting. He was also sailing around the world. He had built a twenty-four-foot steel sloop and was trying to get through the canal and back to Queensland, Australia. He was having a lot of trouble getting funds to allow him to keep traveling. His boat was anchored on The Flats while he tried to arrange passage through the canal. The money had to be sent from Australia to France, and then on to Panama. At that time, France and Australia were having problems about nuclear tests in the Pacific. What ever the problem was, his bank had sent money four times and none had arrived. Because of that, Herme's bank would not send any more money until they found out where the other money had gone.

On many occasions, I fed him meals and bought him beer at the yacht club. One evening, when we were having a beer, he was very excited. It had been storming very hard. We had received lots of rain, wind, and lightning. He needed to check his boat anchor. It had been six hours, and he also wanted to check the bilge. When he arrived at his boat, he found a black mark on the steel deck directly in front of the cabin door. His boat had been hit by lightning, and he had luckily been with me. I finally loaned him some money to continue on his way. I also arranged for him to side-tie to a Columbia 40 to transit the canal. His boat had a small outboard and could not travel fast enough under power to transit the canal alone. I received a lot of razzing from the rest of the crew about loaning money to strangers, but I felt it was the proper thing to do at that time. It was over a year later that I received a nice letter from Herme. He thanked me for trusting him and added extra money for interest. He said that he would have sent it earlier, but he had been dismasted off of the Island of Nauru and had been delayed. He had drifted for two weeks before someone finally rescued him. During that time, he had very little food and only rain water to sustain him. I enjoyed my time with him and he invited me to visit him at any time.

Norm Bennett, the man who towed me to the canal from Isla Grande, was one of those throw-back type of people. He would have been at the Alamo with Davy Crockett if he had been born at that time and in the U.S.A. His big schooner was built in Columbia right on the beach by local craftsman. He told me that the plans for the boat were drawn on the floor of the cottage of the builder. Norm laughed when he told about having to throw the rugs out every time they needed to check the plans. He also told me a wonderful story that I will share with you at this time.

It seemed that Norm had met a man from Honduras who had a large load of Honduras Mahogany lumber for sale. The man was desperate for money, and Norm negotiated a fantastic price on the whole load. He loaded it into the hold of his schooner, and it filled the boat. He was headed from Honduras to Columbia where he would sell the lumber for a nice profit. At the same time, he had to detour to Miami to get some engine parts for someone at the canal and then return to Panama.

When he arrived at Miami, the engine in his boat would not start. He anchored off of Miami Beach, put up his quarantine flag, and waited for U.S. Customs to come and clear him. After twenty-four hours, no one came to check him in, so he jumped into his dingy and rowed to shore. He went into one of the big fancy hotels and asked the clerk at the front desk if he could help him with Customs. He was told that he had to motor up to the Customs Dock to be checked in. He told them that his engine was not running and could not. The desk clerk asked him where he was anchored, and he pointed at his boat anchored directly in front of their hotel. The desk clerk asked him what country that blue flag he was flying represented, and Norm told him that it was the Flag of Columbia.

The desk clerk picked up the telephone and made a short call. Within minutes, a Customs boat arrived and towed Norm's boat to their dock. They accused him of being a drug smuggler, and declared that they were going to search his boat for drugs. Norm told them to go ahead and search. When they saw all of the mahogany, they told him to unload it so that they could search his boat. He told the Customs agents that if they wanted to search his boat, then they would have to unload the boat because he would not. When they asked him about the lumber, Norm told them that he was going to refit his boat with it.

The two Customs agents worked in the hot sun for hours and finally unloaded all of the lumber. They searched his boat and proclaimed that his boat was drug free. When he asked if they were going to put the lumber back into his boat, he was told no, they would not, and said he had two days get the lumber and his boat off of their dock.

Norm went immediately to the local newspaper and placed an advertisement that he had a load of Honduras Mahogany for sale. The next day it was sold at a very large profit. He chuckled as he told me that story. "U.S. Customs thought I was smuggling drugs, and they ended up making me a lumber smuggler."

CHAPTER 6
Drug Dealers

*B*ecause of the monsoon rains, I spent a lot of time in the yacht club keeping my foot dry. I was told to have the dressing changed two or three times a week at the local clinic in Colon, and the safety issue had become much more evident to me. Things were going downhill in Panama at an alarming rate. Each trip to the clinic was taken with Edwin, the security guard, and he would not take no for an answer. We became friends and I will always remember his kindness.

About that time, I met the Commodore of the Panama Canal Yacht Club. His name was Bill Speed, and he was a wonderful man. He and his wife Kay lived on their boat at the yacht club. The boat was

a Peterson 46, with a center cockpit. They had purchased the boat in Taiwan and had sailed it to Panama. They were building a house up the coast near
Isla Grande, and were nice enough to allow Jeff and
Cris to spend some time there. Kay collected charts
from the boaters as they transited the canal and made
them available to boaters headed the other way. She
didn't make any money doing it, but it was just the
right thing to do. That was the way they traveled
through life, being happy and doing the right thing.
They added a lot of joy to an otherwise bad situation.

When the parts arrived, the mechanic started
putting the engine back together. He was working
part time at other places as well, and always had an
excuse for not working on the engine. He eventually
abandoned the project in favor of another job. I could
not be angry at the man for trying to find a better job.
Things were getting difficult for non-Panamanians.

I was getting ready to shut down the trip because of the weather, when a man dressed in a dark
suit asked if he could see my boat. He had heard it
was for sale and said he was interested in buying it.
He said he would be back the next day to look at it.

The next morning, he showed up with another
man also dressed in a dark suit. Now if that sounds

normal, you must remember that it was monsoon season and hot and muggy. They looked over the boat and offered to give me one thousand dollars as a down payment at that time. The boat would have to be ready ASAP. The second man opened his briefcase, and it was full of stacks of one-hundred-dollar bills. He then counted out one thousand dollars, and tried to give them to me.

I was feeling very uncomfortable about this time, so I asked Bill to assist me. Bill took me to one side and informed me that the men were possibly drug dealers. If so, they probably wanted my boat to use as a delivery boat. It would take their drugs up to Miami, Florida to be sold. He also told me that they had offered to buy a Peterson 46 on the same day. It was the boat moored directly in front of me and looked very similar to my boat. I didn't know what to do, but Bill told me to deal with them. They were going to buy two boats, and one might as well be mine. We told them to come by the yacht club on Saturday to close the deal. We would not take their money at this time, but on Saturday we would talk further.

The yacht club was swarming with people on Saturday, and I was quite surprised. Bill had me look around, and then pointed out all of the drug-enforcement officers spread out across the room. I remember thinking to myself, "What have you done? You will probably get yourself shot." Needless to say, the drug dealers did not show up, and it was just another wet day in Panama. We heard the next day that they had purchased two boats that Saturday. While the drug enforcement team was at the yacht club, they had gone to Gatun Lake and had taken delivery on two different boats.

CHAPTER 7
Sending The Crew Home

Norm continued to be of great assistance to me. He had a car and helped me make arraignments to send my crew home to Olympia. I found a boat that needed boat handlers and arranged for Margret, Cris, Gene, and Jeff to transit the canal with them. Norm and I traveled in his car across the isthmus to the Pacific side of the canal. I went to a hotel and made arrangements for lodging and purchased airline tickets for my four, long-suffering crew members.

Then we went to the Panama City Yacht Club on the Pacific side. We were sitting there having a cold beer and thinking about dinner, when I felt soft hands cover my eyes and heard a familiar voice say,

"Remember me? What are you doing on this side of Panama?"

I turned and was surprised to see the young girl who was sailing around the world standing next to me. I was thrilled to see Tania again, and asked her what she was still doing in this horrible place. She said, "I am leaving to continue my trip in the morning. I just wanted to stop and say goodbye." We had a short visit and that was the last time I saw her. I hope I have that privilege again some day. She was someone very special.

As I talked to Norm, another voice, behind me, said hello. I turned and was surprised to see the gentleman I had met at the dock when I first arrived in Panama. It was the man who tried to get me to deliver drugs to Miami. I did not know what to say, so I asked him what he was doing here on this side of the isthmus. He said that he was assigned to watch over the young girl I was talking to. She was his responsibility until she was safely at sea and out of the country. He turned out to be a government law enforcement agent. He stated that he had been watching my boat and had seen the nice things that my crew and I had been doing for the newly arriving boats. It was a nice compliment. While waiting for our engine repairs to be completed, we had made it a point to assist a lot of people in any way we could. We used the knowledge that we had acquired to help the owners and crew members of the other boats. Those were the years of General Noriega, and problems were everywhere. The agent and I were having a very nice talk until he saw Tania start to leave. He quickly excused himself and followed her out the door.

I was amazed that I had been so wrong. My suspected drug smuggler was one of the good guys, and he was aware of everything that my crew and I had done since we arrived in Panama. As I think about it, I think we had been watched the entire time because we had been seen being towed into port by a boat flying a Columbian flag.

Norm and I stayed overnight in a local hotel and left early in the next morning. We traveled back across the isthmus to Cristobal and back to the Panama Canal Yacht Club. My crew was in transit through the canal as boat handlers on one of the sailboats headed west. They would fly home, and their trip would be over. I was glad I had been blessed with such fine friends to help me, and they will always hold a special spot in my heart. Gene has now passed away, and I have lost track of Margret through the years. Jeff went on to become a commercial pilot for a major airline, and I believe it was Alaska Airlines. He and Cris were forced to move out of Olympia because of his job.

CHAPTER 8
Going Home

My trip was over for now. I had been gone for nine weeks, and my office would not allow me any more time off. I was left with only one option, and that was to leave the boat in Panama at the yacht club, come back next year, and try again. I joined the Panama Canal Yacht Club and left the repairs necessary for the boat in the capable hands of Bill Speed. He would get the boat repaired for me and help me arrange for another crew to continue the trip early next year. That would necessitate me getting another leave from work and continuing the trip with a new crew.

I had two more days at the yacht club before I was able to travel back across the isthmus and catch a plane for home. I stayed overnight again, and then I headed for the airport. I had an early flight, and I wanted to be there early.

The boat had been unloaded and everything was stored in lockers at the yacht club. The only things I had with me were my clothes and the ham radio set. I was taking it home to practice on it. It would not be needed in Panama until the following year. The trip was over for now, but I was still ready to carry on. The time would go fast, and besides, what else could happen to me? I had endured more in those nine weeks than anyone I had ever met, and I felt the worst was behind me.

I waited in a preboarding line at the airport for about forty minutes. A woman waved to me and it was my turn at her counter. She asked if I was carrying any foodstuffs or did I have anything purchased to declare? I told her that I just had my clothes and my ham set. I told her that I was carrying it with me. She started shouting at me and said that I had lied to her about not having foodstuffs. I then informed her that I did not lie, and that I only had my clothes and my ham radio. The big box I was carrying had a radio in it.

She called for backup, and a very large man forcibly escorted me to another area. I was told to unpack everything and put each item on the table directly in front of me. That really irritated me, but there was nothing I could do but comply. I was there about another thirty minutes before they would let me repack my bags and the ham radio. I was forced to leave my fingernail clippers behind. I am sure that if I had not mentioned the word *ham*, I would not have had as much trouble. I boarded the plane and was soon headed for Olympia. I felt safe in the knowledge that my trip was over and that next year's trip would be a piece of cake compared to this one. I am ever the optimist. You will see that as I resume my trip next year.

PART TWO

PART TWO

CHAPTER 9
I Start Again

*T*he time was passing by very quickly as I tried to prepare for my return to Panama from my home in Olympia. Each week, I talked with Bill Speed in Panama, and then I sent him the money necessary for repairs on the engine. The repairs to the engine were being done by mechanics working for the Panama Canal Commission. They were working on it in their off hours, and it was a slow process. When additional parts were needed, we either purchased them locally or CSY Yacht Corp. sent them to Panama. This turned out to be a very expensive rebuild, but I had no other options at this time.

I wished that I had been able to purchase a new engine for the boat, but life had continued to bite me when I had least expected it. Bill was also trying to line up a crew in Panama to sail with me on the upcoming trip to Washington, but was having trouble finding qualified crew members. I hoped that it could be resolved soon.

Regarding my job, I had received the okay from my employer to take another nine weeks off in the spring of 1986. That should have been plenty of time to get the boat home. As I wrote this book, I was relying on my memory as a seventy-two-old to write this story the way that it actually happened. To the best of my knowledge, this is an accurate account of the voyage home from Panama.

CHAPTER 10
The Plan

Somewhere around the middle of April, 1986, I boarded an airplane in Seattle and headed back to Panama. I was all excited to be able to continue the trip home to Olympia, Washington from the Panama Canal on my newly refurbished sailboat. I had a slip at the Olympia Yacht Club just waiting for the *El Jay*. The trip on the plane was long and boring. I was unable to sleep because I was too pumped up — thinking about the trip and the wonderful experiences I was going to have. The second trip had to go smoother than the first one because we had a new engine. Bill Speed had successfully completed getting it rebuilt. He had also arranged for a young man named Juan to go on the trip. Bill, with all of his experience as a delivery skipper, also agreed to go along on the trip — positive that the three of us would be enough. I felt honored that the commodore of the Panama Canal Yacht Club thought enough of me to volunteer to assist me and help crew my boat on this long journey back to Olympia. Bill had taken the boat out on a sea trial, and it had performed perfectly. The trip would be a piece of cake, and the pain of the previous trip would be over.

The plan for the trip was to head out toward Hawaii. That path would keep us out of the shipping lanes and give us a knot-and-a-half of current to help push us along. The prevailing winds would also be in our favor. When we got close to Hawaii, we would then turn northeast toward Washington. That would also provide us with the prevailing winds and a knot-and-a-half current. If something went wrong during that time, we could stop in Hawaii to correct whatever the problem was. The plan seemed foolproof, and our days would be spent lazily sailing along or reading. Once we reached Olympia, my crew would board a plane back to Panama. Life would be good and the world would be at peace. Unfortunately, that was the last time I would feel this way. Life has a way of putting dreams into their proper perspective, and the trip was about to do just that.

CHAPTER 11
Transiting the Canal

I arrived in Panama on the Pacific side and had a comfortable train ride across the isthmus to the Panama Canal Yacht Club. Once there, I reacquainted myself with the boat and its surroundings. Bill had been his usual, thorough self. The boat had been loaded with all of the equipment that had been put into storage. The boat looked wonderful, but still weathered. It was late, so I excused myself and went to bed. I was exhausted from the long trip, and needed to allow my body time to adjust to the different time zone.

Most people don't know that the canal entrance on the Pacific side is further east than the Atlantic side. That's right — the canal runs from

Cristobal in the northwest to Panama City in the southeast.

When I got up in the morning, I started doing an inventory of the boat. I was surprised to find many things missing. The boat had been unpacked by three or four local Panamanian workers. It was either them, or the ones who reloaded the equipment back on the boat, that had removed much of the gear. We could not hold anyone accountable and had to buy new equipment to replace what had been stolen. Bill was very upset, but I could not let him take the blame. He had done his best, and that was all anyone could ask for.

The next day was spent going over all of the last-minute details and double-checking the inventory on the boat one more time. Some of the articles stolen that could not be replaced were the mosquito nets. There were none to be had. I could only hope that we would not need them on the trip home. We would be out at sea, and there were no mosquitoes when you got away from shore. I had to think positive about these small problems.

We had the boat hauled out of the water to paint the bottom with antifouling paint and found a problem. The boat had been sitting in saltwater for a whole year. It was normally protected by little pieces of zinc. Those pieces were attached to the metal parts that were below the waterline. The metal pieces were then tied together by metal straps. That makes all of the metal below the waterline one piece. One or two zinc plates can then protect the whole bottom. The common part of this elaborate chain was the engine. Because my engine had been out of the boat so long, electrolysis had made small holes in every blade on the propeller. The drive shaft and all of the through-hull fittings had pits also. It was too late to do anything about that problem at this time, so we painted the bottom and hoped for the best.

Hurricane season was closing in fast, and we could not delay any longer. The boat appeared to be in good shape except for those small problems.

We decide to leave the next day and had a reservation with the Panama Canal Commission to transit the canal. The day was beautiful, and all was right with the world again. Bill and Kay Speed left me and went to their boat to get some sleep. Suddenly, I was startled by someone behind me. It was the man who had originally started to repair my boat engine. He demanded money for the work he had done on the boat. I told him that he had cost me a lot of money by not working on the engine when he had been hired to do so. I explained that I had been forced to shut down the trip and fly all of my crew home, and then hire another crew for the second trip because of him. He threatened me physically, and I ended up giving him money to go away and leave me alone. Welcome to Panama.

The next morning Bill showed up early, and we started to prepare the boat to enter the canal locks. We had to have four 100-foot lines for tying the boat to the sides of the locks. These four lines were then tied to the four corners of the boat and were used to keep the boat centered in each lock. The boat rose in the water as water poured into the lock. Each boat had to have at least four line handlers on the boat and someone to man the wheel because the mixing of sea water and fresh water created a violent turbulence.

In each lock, men would stand at the top and toss down four balls of twine for the crew on the boat to attach each of the four ropes to. The men at the top would then pull the ropes up from the boat and tie them off — looping them around large, round, concrete stays. This would hold each boat in place and keep it from moving.

While we were preparing the boat, the crew started arriving. The crew consisted of myself, Bill, Kay, five nurses from the military hospital where Kay worked (four females and one male), and my new crew member Juan. The man assigned to us from the Panama Canal Commission arrived shortly thereafter.

We were finally on our way, and everyone was laughing and having a good time. We entered the first lock and found ourselves tied along side of a French 32-foot sloop. They could not speak English and we could not understand them either. My boat was larger than theirs, at 46-feet in length, and we tied both boats together at the bow and the stern. We used two of our 100-foot lines for our side of the canal wall, and they used two of their 100-foot lines on their side of the canal wall. Suddenly, the water started to come into the first lock on the Caribbean side of the canal. The turmoil was just unbelievable. Both boats were being thrown from side to side as the water entered the lock, and we started to pull in on the lines. The French boat did also, but the only problem was that they were all excited. They pulled twice as hard as we did, which was quite unnecessary, and this made their boat inch closer to their side of the lock. The lock is solid concrete and will scar any boat very easily if the crew is not careful. They started hollering at us and pointed toward the wall that they were getting close to. We, of course, answered in English that they should probably quit pulling themselves into the wall. We were pulling as hard as the water coming in would allow. If we pulled any harder, we would be trying to lift 38,000 pounds vertically out of the water. That only made them shout louder, and pull harder, and that made their boat get even closer to the concrete wall. We were all laughing so hard by that time that we could hardly pull on our lines to keep us away from the wall. By the time we reached the top of the lock, they could not have had more than a foot of clearance from the wall. It was unbelievable that they were still pulling. That continued in the next set of locks also.

When we reached Gatun Lake, and after exiting the last lock, we slowed down. We wanted to allow that French boat to get far ahead of us. We talked to the man from the Canal Commission, and he said that in his fifteen years he had never seen anybody that dumb.

The trip through the lake was shortened for small boats. The larger ships, like cruise ships, had to travel the whole winding length of Gatun Lake. There was a straighter path for the smaller boats.

The moment we entered Gatun Lake, the music began. One of the nurses had brought a portable radio and put it up on the forward deck. I steered the boat and everyone else went forward and began dancing. The cruise ships near us went crazy. They followed us as long as they could, taking picture after picture. I am probably in at least five-thousand pictures. The trip through the lake was very easy. The man from the Canal Commission was very knowledgeable and very efficient.

We then entered the locks to go down on the Pacific side, and we were relieved to find ourselves alone in the front of the lock. We threw all four 100-foot lines to the men at the top of the lock and waited. Then, we saw what was taking so long. The ship coming up behind us was huge. They had decided to put it in the lock with us. That ship was so huge that it was called a Panamax, and that means that the ship was built to fill the entire lock. That ship, both side to side and end to end, barely cleared the walls of the lock. There was only about a foot on either side. To put that in perspective, the locks are about 108-feet wide and about 1000-feet long, and that ship was over 900-feet long. We had my boat as far forward in the lock as we could safely go, and the big ship just kept on coming. When they finally stopped that huge ship, I was standing on the stern of my boat, looking up at the ship's anchor, and the bow of the ship was almost twenty feet past me. I had the feeling that they could not have squeezed an orange crate between us.

That pattern continued through the remaining two sets of locks. We exited on the Pacific side and proceeded to the dock. We thanked the man from the Panama Canal Commission for his help and dropped him at the dock. Bill said goodbye to his wife Kay, and she and the other crew members were left at the dock and would travel back across the isthmus on the train.

We cast off and headed off into the great unknown called the Pacific Ocean. After leaving the dock, we passed under the bridge of the Americas. In Panama, the Panamanians consider this bridge to be the dividing point between North and South America.

Bill walked over to me and whispered, "I noticed some white smoke coming from the exhaust." That was not good. The engine had been running all day and was completely warmed up. The only time you got white smoke from a diesel was when it's cold, or if water was getting into the engine. The engine was running fine though, but we decided to follow the shoreline for a while just in case it turned out to be a major problem. The white smoke seemed to be disappearing, but we could not go offshore until we were sure.

We sailed along the shore and it was beautiful. The foliage along the coast and on the many islands was spectacular. We decided to stay close to shore and follow the dozens of automated lighthouses scattered among the islands. That would make it easy to travel through the many islands at night. That was a good idea, but none of the lighthouses were working because of poor maintenance. I mean, not one single lighthouse was working. We only had the moon and the compass to help us through the maze of islands. Bill went forward and used hand signals to point in the direction for me to steer the boat.

That was going fine until the rain started, and it got dark. We had to use Juan halfway up the boat to relay signals because I couldn't see Bill, and our hand signals were useless. By the way, did I happen to mention that Juan only spoke Spanish? Did I happen to mention that Bill and I did not?

So here we were in the middle of nowhere, in the dark, and in a driving rainstorm. Was there ever any other kind of night in Panama? We had minimal communication going on. The only thing that made it work was the lightning that illuminated the darkened skies. That allowed me to see Bill. About every five minutes, lightning would strike, and I would see Bill frantically waving his arms, pointing in some direction that I hadn't been going. The depth finder was set for fifteen feet and was constantly howling at us. The sun did not come up too soon for my money, and when it did we all breathed a little easier. We were completely surrounded by little islands, and I don't know to this day how we did it. The Good Lord was watching over us that day. We were all exhausted and needed to rest, so we took turns napping.

We decided to move out into a little deeper water, and that would take the islands out of our way. We also decided to keep following the shore for a few more miles before heading toward Hawaii. Now that we were in deeper water, Juan started fishing.

CHAPTER 12
All About Juan

I **must stop at this time and tell you about** Juan. Juan was only about five-feet-two-inches tall, husky, and about twenty-five-years old. He was from Spain and arrived in Panama on a cargo ship. I hope I have remembered that correctly. He liked Panama and decided to stay for awhile. He had a number of skills, and we hired him to be the diesel mechanic and deckhand. He was one of the nicest young men you would ever meet. Unfortunately, he did not speak English at all. He also had trouble speaking Panama's version of Spanish. All Spanish was not created equal because of the many dialects spoken in the world. I did speak a little Spanish, but very little. Bill did not speak any. In spite of this language barrier, we never shouted at each other unless the wind dictated that it was necessary to raise our voices. We finally settled on a lot of pantomime motions and pointing of fingers. If I wanted to eat and I was at the steering wheel, I would say Juan's name. He would look up, and I would point to my mouth and pretend I was eating. He would laugh and bring me a hammer. He was a very funny young man. After I shook my head no about three times, he would put it down. Then he would pick up a sandwich and bring it to me. He would say, "Que?" It meant, "Was that what you wanted?" That was pretty much how the first few days and nights went. We continued to stay offshore, but still within sight of the shoreline most of the time.

Juan loved to fish. Now that we were out in open water, he always had a fishing line in the water. He had just about 200 feet of eighty-pound-test fishing line, and he wrapped it around one of the winches that wasn't being used. He let it work as a drag would work on a normal fishing reel. It was amazingly simple and effective. He had only been fishing about two hours, when he had already landed a black tuna of about ten pounds. He cleaned it immediately and then disappeared below deck. Very soon, the smell of fish cooking in a frying pan came up from below deck. There were some other smells also, but I did not recognize them.

I was not a fish eater, but that fish was wonderful. He had created his own sauces from scratch, and they were to die for. They were the strange smells that I had previously mentioned. Fishing became an everyday thing, and he would put out a fishing line first thing in the morning. He used homemade lures and did not catch fish every day, but that fish fed us for two days.

On the third day of fishing, he landed a very large fish. I was down below napping, and I heard a very loud noise up in the center cockpit.

When I stuck my head out to see what was going on, I came face to face with a very large wahoo. He looked mad, had big sharp teeth, and he was coming my way. That fish was so heavy and strong that it had straightened the hook on the fishing line. I kicked him back into the cockpit, and Juan secured the fish. I then took a picture of Juan holding his big fish. He had his hand in its gill and held it up next to his head. Juan was not very tall, just over five feet, and the tail of the fish was turned on its side on the cockpit floor. That fish had to be over five-feet-six-inches long and was a beautiful silver color. When the fish was cooked, it was a pure white color, and Juan served it like a steak. He poured a cream-like sauce made from coconut milk on it that was out of this world. By now, you have probably figured out what we were eating for the next seven days. We ate fish and more fish. He finally caught a mahi-mahi of about three pounds. I refused to eat any more fish and ate a ham sandwich. Juan pouted for a while until he finally figured out that I don't like fish. It was a long time before I could eat another piece of fish.

Juan's job was watching the engine very carefully to see if there were any problems, and we seemed to be using a little oil. That engine had just been rebuilt and should not have been using oil. In addition, Juan said that the alternator was getting a little hot and that he would watch it also. Juan was becoming a real asset to the trip. I hoped that I had heard him correctly. Having the engine rebuilt was supposed to be the least of our problems, but things have a way of coming back to bite you sometimes. Little did we know that tomorrow was to be one of those times.

CHAPTER 13
Costa Rica

*T*he trip had been going a little more like I had hoped, and we were getting close to Costa Rica. We made a decision to stop at Puntarenas in Costa Rica. That would give us a chance to rest — while anchored in a safe harbor. We were about two hours from Puntarenas, when the alternator started smoking. We quickly shut down the engine and Juan looked at it. He held up his hands and said "Que?" Then he started taking it off of the engine. We had purchased a spare alternator in Colon, Panama. It was placed on the engine, the engine started, and then the spare went up in smoke also. We disconnected the fan belt, started the engine, and headed for Puntarenas. An auto parts store would be our next stop. We were lucky it was daylight, because a diesel engine doesn't need an alternator to fire any sparkplugs, it's only needed for charging the batteries, lights, and other accessories like the refrigerator/freezer.

When we entered the harbor to Puntarenas, it was very shallow. We were actually in the mouth of a river. We watched all of the boats as they went up the river. We noticed that they all stayed to the right side of the channel, and we followed them right up to Puntarenas, keeping to the right, without any problem at all. We anchored with the rest of the sailboats, and Juan and I went to shore in the dingy. We had both alternators with us and hoped to find someone to repair them. We also had to find the Port Captain's Office to check in.

We were walking down the street looking for help, but nobody spoke English, and they could not understand Juan's brand of Spanish. We were getting frustrated, and I noticed someone had been following us. That was a very dangerous town, and we had been warned to be careful. Finally, the man following us tugged at my shirt. I told him to go away, and that I didn't want to buy anything. He persisted, and then Juan told him to go away. He understood Juan, and reached into his pocket. I thought he was going to pull out a gun, but instead he pulled out a policeman's badge. He told Juan that he was the Chief of Police in Puntarenas, and we had to go with him to the Port Captain's Office. Juan did all of the talking, and after I had seen the police badge and gun, I just followed Juan.

We walked about ten blocks and arrived at the Port Captain's Office. The Port Captain was very angry at first. He spoke very good English and said that I should have come to his office immediately upon arriving in the harbor. I informed him that we had been trying to find his office, and that nobody we had met along the way spoke English, except him. I also told him that Juan spoke Spanish, but nobody could understand his dialect. He turned to the Chief of Police and spoke to him in Costa-Rican Spanish. Neither Juan nor myself could understand them, but he must have heard what he wanted from the police chief. He turned to me and said, You need a permit to stay for the next five days." I told him that we were just here to get repairs and then would be on our way. He informed me that five days is the minimum amount of the permit to anchor. He asked for my Zarpe. I handed it to him and a copy of my Crew List.

This seemed to make him happy. He made a few telephone calls, and then he smiled and said, "Both of you come with me." He had a Datsun pickup truck that had seen its better days, and I hopped into the front seat next to him. There was no room for anyone else, as he was a very fat man. Juan and the policeman hopped into the bed of the pickup. The Port Captain started the engine, and off we went. He drove about two miles and then stopped. "We must get the Customs Man," he said. He honked the horn and another large man appeared. After a brief conversation between him and the Port Captain, he climbed into the bed of the pickup with Juan and the policeman. Off we went again, traveling down another dusty road. The truck stopped again, and again the horn was honked.

I asked, "What now?"

"I have to pick up the Immigrations Man," he said.

I informed him at that time that I was not trying to settle in his country. I only wanted to fix my alternator. The Port Captain said, "They all must sign your permit." We loaded that man into the back of the truck, and then proceeded on down the road to the boat.

When we arrived at the dock, a Costa-Rican naval vessel was waiting to take us out to my boat. We all boarded the naval vessel, a twenty-two-foot open boat, and headed for the *El Jay*. The man running the boat had many different insignias on his uniform and looked to be a very high-ranking officer. We boarded my boat and Bill looked surprised. He pulled me to one side and said that the permit was only supposed to cost fifteen dollars American. I said, "I think they have something else in mind."

The Port Captain sat down at the table in the main cabin and looked at me. He said, "Today is Saturday, and that is an overtime day, so give me 120 dollars American."

I gave him six twenty-dollar bills. The Port Captain gave one twenty-dollar bill to each of the men with him — one for the policeman, one for the Customs Man, and one for the Immigration Man. He put the other sixty dollars in his own pocket, smiled, and said, "I am the boss."

About that time, I heard a loud crash from up on deck. I looked out through the hatch and saw a huge man sprawled on the deck. He looked up at me and yelled, "Customs." At least that is what I thought he said. He was so drunk, he could hardly stand and had fallen over the rail and down into the center cockpit.

Bill told Juan to throw him overboard, but the Port Captain said, "No. Give me twenty dollars more." I asked him what for? I explained that I already had a Customs Man onboard. "To get your permit," he said. I am probably the only person that you will ever meet who paid $140 for a $15 permit. I was glad to feel such a warm welcome in Costa Rica.

We spent the next three days in Puntarenas. We repaired the boat and picked up a spare alternator. I did a little local sightseeing and decided to try some of the local food. It was breakfast time, and I was hungry for bacon and eggs. I stopped at a local café where the local people were eating. I sat down and looked at the man seated next to me. "Se habla Englesa?" (do you speak English?) I asked.

"Pequito," (a little) he said. I asked him what he was eating, and pointed to his eggs. "Huevos," (eggs) he replied. I pointed at his beans and asked him what that was. "Frejoles negros," (black beans) was his reply.

The next item on his plate was the most puzzling. It looked like meat, but it was gray. I had never seen gray meat before. I asked him, "Que?" (what?) and pointed to the gray material on his plate.

He said in English, "Meat." I was surprised, and I asked him what kind of meat it was. He just shook his head and said, "Meat." I looked around and noticed that there were no animals around — no monkeys chattering in the jungle — and no dogs or cats. I had not even seen a rat. The waitress came to get my order and I proudly ordered in Spanish. "Huevos, frijoles negros, nada meat."

CHAPTER 14
Travel by Zarpe

At this time, I will tell you about travel by boat between Central-American and South-American countries. When you travel by boat, you must get a Zarpe from the Port Captain's Office from your point of origin. This is a piece of paper listing all of the places that you might stop at during your trip, and your final destination. You are not allowed to stop or go ashore at any other places. These are places where you are allowed to stop, but you are not required to stop at any of them except your final destination.

You must also present four copies of a Crew List. The Port Captain at your point of origin will keep three of them and return the fourth one to you. Both the Zarpe and the Crew List will be stamped with the date, the time of day, and the official seal of that port office. The list consists of a sheet of paper with the names of all of the people on your boat.

When you get to any one of the stops listed on the Zarpe and stay for any length of time, you must report to the Port Captain's Office at that location. He will take the Zarpe and the Crew List. When you leave, you must start the whole process all over again, and now your port of origin is that port and your Crew List is new from that moment on. You can also change all stops and your final destination at this time, if you wish.

The Port Captain will not stamp any passport, even though he will ask to see everyone's passport. They also will not issue you a visa to be in the country. You can only stay for the time specified on the permit which he will issue to you. This process is so cumbersome that you try to limit the numbers of stops that you list on each Zarpe. You must list some stops that will not be visited because of potential emergences. The first stop at each port of call is the Port Captain. Customs will sometimes come out to your boat if you fly a quarantine flag.

When you travel by airplane or automobile, you must have a passport. If you are staying for any length of time, you must have a visa. These government officials will stamp your passport, and they will not accept a Zarpe for anything. This is true for a copy of the Crew List also.

CHAPTER 15
Heavy Weather Ahead

We were preparing to leave Puntarenas, and I was approached by a young Mexican named Nouyo. He was from Zihuatanejo, Mexico. He had been traveling on a boat from his hometown, and they had run into engine trouble. He was out of money and could not get back home. He asked if he could sail with us to his hometown in Mexico. I told him that he could come along, but he would have to work without wages. He was just glad to be in a safe place and said yes immediately. The main reason I accepted his offer was, he had been recommended to me by another boat that I had met in Panama. He also spoke both English and Spanish, however, the latter did not work out well at first. Nouyo and Juan had difficulty understanding each other. It took them about three days of jabbering at each other before they were very comfortable with their common language.

We left Puntarenas and headed north, confident that our language problems had been solved for the moment. The rest of the trip would be a breeze, and the U.S.A. would be the last country listed on the Zarpe, with only the Mexico stops in between. San Diego was looking very good about now. The next country on our trip to sail past was Nicaragua, and we were not allowed to stop there and didn't want to. The war between the Contras and the U.S.A.-backed federal government was in full swing, and Americans were not welcome by the rebels.

On the northern coast of Costa Rica is a large bay called the Golfo de Papagayo (Gulf of Papagayo). To save time, we decided not to sail close to the shore and travel along the coast of the bay, and instead we headed straight across the open water where the gulf met the Pacific Ocean. This whole area was famous for bad storms in the hurricane season, and this time was no different.

It was about midnight when we felt the first winds. Bill and Nouyo were sleeping, and I was relieving Juan at the wheel. Juan decided to stay up for a little longer because the air was cooler on deck and too warm below in the cabin, and that turned out to be a good decision for what was about to set upon us.

The wind increased very quickly and soon, within an hour, it was howling. The wind had come out of nowhere. It was typical of the area. You could not even see it coming, especially at night.

We had to get those sails down — fast. Juan was standing right next to me, and I turned and asked him to wake Bill and Nouyo, explaining that he would need help lowering all of the sails. I kept the engine running and the boat headed into the wind to take the wind out of the sails, but the waves were now pushing us toward the rocks onshore. The little diesel engine was working as hard as it could, but it could not keep up with the tremendous force of all of those waves — hitting the side of the boat — pushing us sideways. We were in less than a hundred feet of water, and it was getting more and more shallow as we got closer and closer to the rocky shore.

Bill and Nouyo started dropping the sails, and it was almost impossible for them to keep their footing on the tossing deck. Juan had the anchor ready and waited for me to tell him if we were in shallow enough water. When the water was fifty-feet deep, we would have the proper scope on the anchor line to anchor without getting swung around and grounding on the rocks. We would have to drop the anchor and wait out the storm, which we did.

All of the sails got safely rolled up and stowed on deck except the main. It was reefed and was as small as it could be without taking it down completely. That helped stabilize the boat against the waves created by the winds gusting across the ocean. The rain appeared to be driven by hurricane-strength gusts, and it felt like sharp needles were stabbing me all over my exposed body. I had experienced the feeling of this type of rain on my skin driven by hurricane-force winds once before during Hurricane David in the Virgin Islands.

The swells from this storm were about fifteen-feet high and were coming in one after the other — in rapid succession — and all we could do was hold on for dear life. The wind blew fiercely for about two straight hours, and then let up as quickly as it had started.

We were battered, but not broken, and we ate a light meal as we headed north toward Nicaragua.

That had been tough, but we had survived and believed things could only get better. The rain and air had been very cold during the storm, but now that the storm had passed, the weather was warm. The fish were biting again, and the boat was performing perfectly.

We then sailed into Nicaraguan waters. We were playing it safe and staying well offshore — we couldn't even see land — when we looked straight northward and saw a wall of water coming at us. It looked to be about ten-feet tall and covered the entire northern horizon. As it came closer, we became very apprehensive. It looked like a ten-foot-high log about four miles long, and it was coming right down our throats. I was at the wheel and had no idea what this was, but it was coming right at us.

I prepared for the worst, and my crew had recognized the threat as well and started to lower the sails. We would hit whatever it was head on, so we slowed our speed to two knots and waited. The wall came closer and closer, and then it split into pieces. It turned out that it was made up of hundreds or thousands of some kind of dolphin, and they were everywhere. They played around the boat for hours — and they seemed as surprised to see us out there in the ocean — as we were to see them. They followed us for over an hour, jumping and racing around the boat, and then turned and headed southward on their original course — known only to them.

When were almost out of Nicaragua, on our way to the coast of El Salvador, we started to breathe easier. But life was still not through with us. It was getting dark, and the fan belt on the engine shredded and broke into many small strips. We were going to have to shut the engine off to add a new belt, and we wanted to be anchored when we did it.

We headed for the Nicaraguan shore in the black of night with no moon and an overcast sky. We did not have permission to land in Nicaragua, but we had no other choice. The Contras controlled most of the area we were in and that made it a bad situation even worse. We could not see anything, and had to depend on the depth finder to lead us to shore.

We hit the fifty-foot mark and dropped the anchor. We were in quiet water, and we were all tired. Tomorrow would be a better time to fix the engine. We set up shifts and went down for the night. We made sure that all lights were extinguished. We did not need to advertise our presence to the unknown onshore. The night was short, and we knew that we had to get going at first light.

At dawn, we were surprised to find ourselves surrounded by about twenty small, open, wooden boats. They were all very badly weathered. We did not know if they were being used or if they had been abandoned. The area onshore looked deserted and looked like some kind of a fruit processing plant set up in an orchard-like setting.

If it was deserted there had to be a reason, and we did not want to wait around and find out what it was. Juan put a new fan belt on the engine as quickly as he could, and I waited for him to signal that it was all right to start the engine. Everyone was nervous about the noise that the engine would make when it started, and we made preparations to pull the anchor as soon as possible. Juan waved, and I tried to start the engine. The batteries were so low from using the lights and running the refrigerator-freezer the night before, and also from running the engine for a while without a fan belt, that I could not get the engine to start.

Bill switched to the back-up bank of batteries, but the engine still would not turn over fast enough to start. Everybody was getting nervous because were making noise and might be attracting unwanted attention, but our luck was holding and nobody came looking for us. I got into my personal bag of tools and found a meter to measure the batteries. Once I uncovered them, I could test them and look for the problem.

The boat had two banks of batteries, each consisting of two huge, six-volt batteries. They were the kind that would be found in a forklift and were very heavy. The batteries were pretty well shot and would have to be replaced as soon as possible. I wired all four of them together, and that was enough to get the engine going.

We pulled anchor and got out of there as quickly as we could, constantly apprehensive about the possibility of gunfire erupting from behind the trees on the shore. I am sure that if the Contras had seen us, they would have captured us, and they would have made life very unpleasant.

We breezed past the rest of Nicaragua, sailed past a tiny stretch of Honduras, and also past El Salvador without a hitch — but we did not dare shut the engine off for fear that it would not start again. I checked the batteries every day, and they would still not hold a charge. If the engine died, we were at the mercy of the sails and the wind.

Juan became his usual, happy self during this part of the journey, and the meals he prepared were incredible. He would make different sauces for each meal, and they were to die for. He and Nouyo were both a joy to have on board, but without Nouyo's ability to speak English and Spanish, it would have been quite different.

Bill was one of the most polished and confident men that I have ever met, and I am sure that his attitude helped the younger men through the trying times that we had been having. I was having a ball, and this was the adventure of a lifetime. I was living it instead of reading about it, and I was in seventh heaven. Some of the experiences had been a little extreme, but I was still alive and the boat was still headed north.

Guatemala passed by without any problems, and the little engine still putted along just fine. The sails were full, and the boat was performing perfectly. If everything went as smooth as this part of the trip, we would have smooth sailing all the way to Puerto Madero. That was the first port listed on the newest version of our Zarpe where we could legally stop.

We crossed the border of Mexico and breathed a sigh of relief. We were now safe from the wars that were affecting Nicaragua, Honduras, El Salvador, and Guatemala. We were just a short distance from Puerto Madero, and the boat was cruising along at a speed of six knots. We were safe for the moment and hoped that the engine would keep running until we reached a safe and secure harbor.

Juan had been sleeping down below and hollered up to the deck. "I hear loud noises coming from the engine." Bill pulled the cover off of the engine compartment, and we could see water spraying from the water pump all over the engine. That engine was cooled by saltwater, and the engine was covered with it. We built a metal shield to deflect the saltwater, but we knew that would be a temporary fix. We were about fifteen miles from Puerto Madero without a spare, and we could only hope it lasted that long. We would arrive during the daytime at about noon, and that would be in our favor.

Finding a water pump to fit our engine would be a different problem. Nouyo hollered for me to stop the boat, and I turned to see a huge Mexican Cruiser about two miles off our stern. I asked him if wanted me to stop. He said, "They are lowering a boat over the side and probably want to check us out."

Bill told me that that was their problem, and we had problems of our own. We decided against stopping and continued on toward Puerto Madero, hoping they would not hold us up. We needed to get anchored before dark.

Sure enough, they pulled alongside of us in a Boston Whaler of about twenty feet. Bill was at the wheel and never slowed the boat.

They boarded us while we were traveling at six knots. They asked for our papers and made sure that we noticed their automatic weapons. After they checked our documents, they got back into their Boston Whaler and headed back to their Mexican Cruiser.

Then they followed us all the way to Puerto Madero. As we entered the main channel toward our anchorage, a different, small, naval boat came alongside and tried to get us to follow them. I was at the wheel and told Nouyo to tell them that it looked too shallow for us to go where they wanted us to go.

I headed straight for the main anchorage and anchored right in the middle of about thirty other boats. I had been told stories about some of the problems encountered by other sailors and thought there would be safety in numbers.

Immediately after we anchored, an official-looking, small boat pulled alongside of us.

Three military men boarded the *El Jay* with automatic weapons in their hands. The lead man was about five-feet tall and had military braid all over his uniform. He had a cocky swagger to his walk which put me on guard. He was mad at me for not going where they wanted me to go with the boat. He told Nouyo to send me and Juan to the bow of the boat. Nouyo and Bill were told to stay in the center cockpit. A military man with an automatic weapon stood guard on Juan and me in the hot, Mexican, noonday sun. We stood there with his automatic weapon pointed at my midsection for about two hours.

The head of the military quizzed Bill, and Nouyo translated Spanish to English and back again. There was a lot of shouting between Bill and the military personnel. Bill had been an officer in the U.S. Navy and was very sure of himself. He did not like little Napoleon types. I don't care for them very much myself.

A mosquito landed on my arm, and without thinking, I swatted at it. The slap made a loud noise. The man pointing the automatic weapon at me appeared to be getting sleepy and had let his weapon droop down a little bit, but when he heard that slap it came up in a hurry with his finger on the trigger and his eyes wide open.

"Mosquito! Mosquito!" I hollered at him. He thought for a moment, and then he smiled and lowered his weapon. That was a very interesting situation to be in, and I remember it with some apprehension to this day. About that time, I heard shouting from the main cabin. Then, after a short silence, I heard very loud laughing by the military men. Still laughing, they came up on deck, boarded their boat, and left.

Bill was still smiling and Nouyo looked as white as a sheet — as if he was going to throw up. When I asked Bill what had just happened here, this is what he told me. "The little guy and his assistant were tearing into everything on the boat. They even pulled the moldings off of the cabin doors. They completely destroyed the forward cabin, and they were tearing up the main cabin as well. I kept hollering at them to stop. The Mexicans could not speak English, and would not listen to me unless Nouyo translated for me. They finally got to the two big bags of flour that we were holding for emergencies, and told Nouyo to slice them open. I told Nouyo not to do that. I told them that they were only bags of flour and were not drugs. The little, Napoleon-type military man grabbed a knife and sliced one of the bags open and was about to slice the other one when I yelled at him, telling him to stop doing that, light the oven, and start baking bread. We have a rule on this boat that whoever opens a bag of flour, for whatever reason, must bake loaves of bread. Now it's your turn. Nouyo did not want to translate that for me, but I insisted. Nouyo told him what I said and the little gentleman looked at me and started laughing. He then turned and left the boat. I think this will be his favorite story for the month." I started to laugh myself because I would have done the same thing.

I remember asking Bill why the Mexican military was being so hard on us. They had pursued us with a Navy Light Cruiser and had torn the boat apart. This was the answer he gave me.

"Everyone in drug enforcement at the Panama Canal knew you and that you had been approached by drug dealers about buying your boat. You abruptly took it off of the market and left the country. Then you come back to Panama, and the drug dealers are looking for new boats to replace the ones purchased last year. You sneak into the country for one day and quickly leave with a new crew.

"Now, let's talk about the crew. I am a six-foot-four-inch-tall delivery skipper. I have delivered many boats through the years. I am also an African-American, and we live in a prejudiced world. Your new crew member is a Spaniard who only speaks Spanish and has an excellent knowledge of the local waters around Panama. Your boat is very voluminous, which is what the drug dealers use for smuggling. You are the white moneyman here to handle all of the financial transactions. Ronald Reagan is the new U.S. President and is pushing Mexico to stop the flow of drugs into the U.S.A. We sneak around through the local islands, in the middle of a storm, with no lighthouses working, stay close in, tight to the coastline, and wind up in Costa Rica. There we meet a Mexican.

"Nouyo had just traveled down from Mexico and knows the local waters between Costa Rica and Mexico. He would be the one who helped us sneak along the coast and into Nicaragua. It would be assumed that we either loaded or offloaded when we anchored overnight.

"Then we continued to sneak along the coast and under the radar until we arrived in Mexico. Once there, we wouldn't go to the naval docks, but try to hide among the private yachts anchored in the bay. It must be assumed by the Mexican government that we were up to something. Now, if I was telling you that story about another boat, what would you think that boat was doing?"

I thought for a moment and realized that we did indeed look and act like smugglers. We fit the profile perfectly.

We couldn't find a spare water pump anywhere in the small village. We questioned the other boats in the anchorage, and one of them had a spare that we were able to adapt and make fit. While we were doing all of that, the local villagers were racing their boats all around us. That went on for one whole day. We thought that it was very rude for them to stir up the water and make the boats rock for no reason. When we asked the owner of the boat that had sold us the water pump about it, we were sorry we had been so upset.

It turned out that ten Pongas (small open fishing boats about twenty-feet long, with a single outboard engine, and about fifteen gallons of fuel) had been blown out to sea in a bad storm. There had been fifteen fishermen in the ten Pongas, and they were all feared lost. That type of storm, which comes from the Gulf of Mexico and blows across the isthmus and into the Gulf of Tehuantepec, could blow a boat 300 miles out to sea — and with such a small fuel supply — they would not be able to get back. They would eventually die out there in the hot sun without fuel, food, or water. We were visibly moved to tears at the thought of it, and we all vowed to be a little more tolerant after that.

The new water pump was adapted by putting a hose within a hose, thereby making the opening small enough to slip snugly onto our engine. The repairs were completed in about two hours.

The Mexican Government seemed to be satisfied with us and did not hinder us anymore. We were anchored safely at Puerto Madero, and had been able to purchase new batteries in the local village, however, we had to wait three days for the stores to open because it had been a three-day holiday — Cinco de Mayo. The new water pump was working perfectly, and the engine was running quietly. The new batteries were holding their charge like they were supposed to. We were rested, and except for a few minor problems, the boat was finally back in order. It was too late to leave until the next day, so we decided to turn in early and leave in the morning. Everything that could happen — had happened — and the remainder of the trip should be wonderful. Hadn't I said that before?

We got up the next morning and then decided to stay in Puerto Madero for a few more days. We had celebrated Cinco de Mayo with the locals and were enjoying the little village. We also decided to fix the other small problems that had been annoying.

Bill and I decided to visit the area that the military had tried to steer us to when we arrived. It was a naval area made up of docks and warehouses. At one of the docks, there was an abandoned hull of a boat. Bill thought it looked like a Chinese Junk. That triggered a memory, and I quickly checked the name on the stern of the boat. If my memory serves me right, the name was *Wind Song*. I had heard about that boat and needed to talk to Nouyo. Sure enough, when we returned to the *El Jay*, he remembered it also.

There was a bar/restaurant in Costa Rica that all of the boaters used. They had a bulletin board for messages that could be left for boats that were coming and going. Posted on the board, there had been a request for information on a Chinese Junk named *Wind Song*. It had been stolen and the owner wanted to find it. When we saw it at the military dock, it had been completely disassembled and was a worthless hull. I have no doubt that the *El Jay* would have suffered the same fate if I had allowed them to lead me to that graveyard.

The rest of the time passed swiftly, and everything seemed to be in good working order. We decided, once again, to head out to sea in the morning. Hurricane season had moved into full swing now, and because of our delays, this put us at risk for the first hurricane of the season. Every day, it got more dangerous to be at sea, and we knew it. What we did not know, however, and had no way of knowing because of the lack of news in that village, was that the first hurricane had already started to build — way out in the Pacific — as we resumed our trip. Where we were when we departed, the weather was sunny and there was just a trace of clouds in the sky to the north of us. The *El Jay* was finally nearing the last leg of her journey home.

The Golfo de Tehuantepec (Gulf of Tehuantepec) was a very dangerous stretch of water. Hurricanes spawned in the Gulf of Mexico have passed over the small isthmus and wreaked havoc in the Gulf of Tehuantepec. Storms that naturally occurred in the Pacific Ocean also collided there on the coast as they headed north toward the Sea of Cortez. We had learned our lesson in the previous storm in the Gulf of Papagayo. This time, we decided to follow the shoreline around the Gulf of Tehuantepec, just to play it safe.

We had sailed about halfway around the gulf, and things could not have been smoother.

About midnight, it was my turn to go on watch to relieve Juan. The wind had started to increase in velocity, enough that Juan was concerned, and he decided to stay up on deck and sleep in the center cockpit next to me. He had barely fallen asleep when the weather took a violent turn for the worse. We were in fifty feet of water and the swells were suddenly very close together. Juan roused Bill and Nouyo and they started taking down all of the sails — including the main — as fast as they could, working with flashlights in the pitch-black of the night. We readied the boat for a big storm and proceeded to inch in toward shore.

The wind was blowing across the isthmus and trying to blow us out to sea. We anchored the boat — tight — in close to shore, and prayed that the wind would not change direction and blow us onto the beach. We had set two anchors and had kept the engine running to keep tension on the anchor lines, waiting for the full impact of the storm.

The storm building out at sea had developed into a full-blown hurricane. Initially, it had been headed south and would have been no threat to us. But it suddenly — and totally — reversed direction and came right at the shore near Acapulco. Then it switched directions again — the eye heading southeast right down the coast — and coming right at us. The outer winds from the hurricane circled over the isthmus into the Gulf of Mexico, and then came back at us from across the isthmus like a freight train.

It hit us hard, and there was nothing we could do but hold on for dear life and pray. Both anchors held as the storm raged and tried to dislodge us from the beach. Someone had to man the wheel and steer the boat constantly — while others had to watch the anchors — because if one of them pulled loose, we had to know immediately so we could try to reset it. It was exhausting and seemingly unending. We switched turns at the wheel often, and many times heard the words, "I'm too tired. Someone else has to do it. Please."

We all knew that if the winds shifted and came at us from the west, this would have twisted the anchors loose and pulled them out — there would have been no time to reset them — and we would have quickly been in too shallow of water to reset them anyway. We would have been thrown onto the shore and probably would have died in the heavy surf. It was an extremely dangerous situation to be in, and all we could do was work our hardest and pray. The rain came down in sheets and at us at an angle because of the high wind, and we felt like we were standing under a horizontal waterfall. The storm dropped ten inches of rain on both sides of the isthmus as we rode it out in the *El Jay*.

In the middle of this terrible storm, my thoughts suddenly went back to the villagers of Puerto Madero and how the fishermen had been lost at sea in that bad storm. I could not help but wonder if this was to be my fate and the fate of my crew as well. I looked at my crew, each of them, and saw the doubt as it flitted across their faces. Life suddenly took on a new meaning, and I knew that if I survived this storm that God was watching over me. The storm lasted for many hours, but the winds never shifted to come from the west, and we had managed to stay safely off the beach. Both of the anchors had held and the engine kept running through the whole ordeal. When the storm finally subsided, we felt exhausted, blessed, and relieved.

The Papagayo had been a bad storm, but it had only had hurricane-strength gusts. This storm was a full strength, category-one hurricane. After researching data back home, the storm was Hurricane Agatha, a storm with sustained winds at a high of 75mph. The time frame, May 20, 1986 to May 29, 1986 fits the profile of our journey perfectly. We had been in it, whether we liked it or not.

We continued on our way and then noticed that the exhaust from the engine was a little more black than before. This was a strong indication that the engine would fail again. Knowing this, we knew that we would never be able to head out to sea and were destined to stay close to shore for the remainder of the trip. We were exhausted and needed rest. We proceeded around the shore — heading for Salina Cruz. Once there, we could safely anchor in protected waters and get some much-needed rest. The hurricane had completely drained us — physically — and emotionally.

Salina Cruz (it is now called Huatulco and a major cruise ship destination) was a sleepy little village and a port for shrimp boats. We tied up next to a shrimp boat and ordered fuel from one of the locals. While he was adding fuel to the boat from a fifty-five gallon drum, we broke out the cold beer that we had been saving. It was about ten o'clock in the morning, but it was happy hour somewhere in the world, and that was good enough for us after what we'd been through.

The shrimp boat next to us was twenty feet higher to their deck. We looked up and saw three people standing at the rail looking down at us. They began to talk to us, and Nouyo said that they wanted a beer also. We tossed each one of them one beer and saluted them by raising ours and then taking a sip. They laughed and did the same.

Later in the day, they offered to share their fish dinner with us. They held up a stiff-as-a-board and dried-out fish to show us what was for dinner. We politely declined and were then presented with another offer. The woman would be available to each of us for another beer. It's amazing what a cold beer will bring in a hot climate. We looked at the woman standing there, and she seemed very shy. We smiled and politely declined that offer also, and said that our wives would not be very understanding. They smiled back at us and proceeded to fix their dinner. We never saw them again.

We left early the next morning, and the sun was already shining brightly. We raised our sails and prepared for a nice sail as we headed northwest along the coast toward Acapulco. We had been running about two hours, when Juan looked behind the boat and hollered for me to stop the engine. He had seen excessive black smoke coming out of the exhaust and wanted to check the engine oil level.

I slowed the boat by turning into the wind, and that allowed the sails to go slack. I turned the engine off and Juan checked the oil level. We were down over a quart. The engine had started to burn oil at an alarming rate. We had purchased plenty of oil in advance, in fifteen, five-gallon cans strapped to the side of the boat, just in case the engine used oil after the rebuild. We were lucky we had done this and also that it had not been ripped off the side of the boat during the hurricane. The engine had not needed any extra oil until now, and from this point on, adding oil to the crankcase would be necessary until we made it to Acapulco, if we made it at all.

The rest of the trip to Acapulco was spent with nerves on edge and a feeling of dread. The engine was running fine, but was burning oil fast and the trip was threatened by failure once again. We sailed most of the time and only used the engine to recharge the batteries, keep the refrigerator/freezer cold, or for emergencies. This slowed the speed of the *El Jay* down considerably because we were sailing into a knot-and-a-half current. Once we got used to adding oil at regular intervals, the trip continued as before — all the way to Acapulco.

We arrived at the Port of Acapulco and tied up to the visitor dock. Juan started checking out the engine, and Bill and I went immediately to the Port Captain's Office. Our Zarpe had expired because this was the final destination listed on it, and it allowed us to go no further without renewing it.

Acapulco is a very large city and the busiest port on the west coast of Mexico. If we had a breakdown, this was the best place to be, other than somewhere in the U.S.A. We were exploring our options regarding the engine problem, and this was the place to find them. Everything would be available, just like in the U.S.A. All we wanted to do was make sure that we would not break down on the way to San Diego or Los Angeles. We were weary from the language barrier and looked forward to being rid of it.

Juan checked the engine, and said that we had been burning oil at a very high rate. He changed the oil and said that he thought the boat could continue on its way and make it to a port in the States. By boat, it should only take us one week to cross the Gulf of California to Cabo San Lucas from Acapulco, and one additional week to get to San Diego.

I made the decision to get off the boat in Acapulco and fly to the Los Angeles area immediately. Once there, I would arrange for spare parts and/or a rebuild kit from the factory. This would provide us with the necessary parts in case we needed to work on the engine at some other point along the way. I just didn't want to risk going any further without having parts available for me to bring by air to the *El Jay*. This would protect us if the boat engine problems became any worse between Acapulco and Cabo San Lucas. I would bring the necessary parts to Cabo San Lucas if necessary. They were expected to arrive in Cabo, hopefully, within a week. If they could not proceed with the trip from there, they would call me and tell me. If I didn't receive a phone call, then it was agreed that everything was OK, and they would continue along their way and meet me in San Diego. My crew was given the telephone number of my friend, Byron

Chamberlain. He lived in Newport Beach, California. I would be staying there with him, awaiting their call.

Bill and I went to the Port Captain's Office and filed three copies of the new Crew List, minus me, and received a new Zarpe listing San Diego as the terminating point. Cabo San Lucas was the only other stop listed on the Zarpe. I kept a copy of the old Crew List for myself.

When we entered Mexico, they would not stamp our passports like Costa Rica had. Because of that, when I left on the airplane from Acapulco to Los Angeles by way of Mexico City, all I had for documentation was my passport and a copy of the old Crew List with my name on it. Little did I know that I would run into a snag changing airplanes in Mexico City because of that.

As I watched the boat sail away without me, I felt both relief and sorrow. The crew had become like family and the boat a second home. I felt abandoned in a foreign land, and my escape was headed out to sea without me. Once they had disappeared from view, I grabbed my bags, hailed a cab, and headed for the airport.

CHAPTER 16
Leaving My Crew

The airport in Acapulco was very modern compared to most other countries. After a few minor delays, I was on my way to Los Angeles, but first I had a change of airplanes in Mexico City.

I arrived in Mexico City and had a two-hour wait for my flight. I would be leaving about 4:00 PM with a direct flight to Los Angeles, and my bags were already on the airplane. I was almost asleep in a chair when a young man asked me to accompany him to the ticket counter. He spoke very good English, and that was a relief. Using the young man as an interpreter, the clerk at the counter asked me for my visa to be in Mexico, and I said I did not have one. He asked for my passport and after checking it, he informed me that I did not have a stamp in it showing that I had arrived in Mexico.

I went through the whole story about coming into the country by boat and not being able to get my passport stamped. I showed him a copy of the Crew List, and pointed to the official stamp of the Port Captain. I was informed that I could not fly out of the country without showing a visa and having a stamped passport showing entry. When I asked what other choices I had, I was told to go back to Acapulco and get back on my boat. I told him that his suggestion would not be possible because the boat had already left for Cabo San Lucas ten hours before. He told me that he didn't care and would not talk to me anymore. They took my bags off of the airplane and left me standing there with no answers to any of my problems.

The young man who had awakened me was standing next to me and started to walk away as well. I stopped him and asked him, "Will you please help this Gringo and tell me what to do? I will give you fifty dollars if you help me."

He smiled at me, patted my shoulder, and said that he would. He took me directly to the boss of the counter clerk, and we were given the same answer.

This stupidity continued until I was talking to the head of that same department for Mexico City and all of Mexico. His answer was the same, and he walked off with an indignant huff. I was beside myself with this bureaucratic nightmare, and this was the solution my helper came up with. "You must change your flight to travel to Tijuana, Mexico. There you will be able to walk across the border and into the U.S.A. In Mexico, the bureaus that regulate travel within Mexico don't talk to each other. They run their little worlds the way they want to, and if you come in by boat you had better leave by boat. This means a Zarpe and the Crew Lists. If you come in by airplane, you need a visa and to have your passport stamped. This problem happens all of the time."

He then helped me change my airplane tickets for a flight to Tijuana by way of La Paz, Mexico. The flight to La Paz did not leave until 8:00 AM the next morning, so I was stuck sitting up all night in a chair in the Mexico City Airport. I tried to sleep a little, but when I did, people kept trying to steal my bags and my airline ticket. I would feel something in my shirt pocket which would awaken me suddenly, and it would be someone's hand trying to take my airline tickets and passport. I would slap their hand away and grab my tickets. This happened more than once. I also had to put my feet on my bags so that if they grabbed those, my feet would fall down and wake me up again. One man who grabbed them saw me wake up and said in Spanish, "Oh, excuse me," expecting me to believe that he had merely tripped over them and my feet. Needless to say, it was a long and dangerous night.

The next morning I boarded a Mexicana Airlines DC10 aircraft and headed for La Paz. I fell asleep immediately and did not feel the airplane touch down in La Paz. I was awaken by a cabin steward and told to deplane immediately. I informed him that I was not getting off in La Paz, but in Tijuana. He told me that they had a bomb on board and I needed to get off. I asked him how they knew that there was a bomb on board, and was told that there were more bags than passengers, and that meant there was a bomb on board.

I was led to a small terminal and jammed in with about 230 other people. We were held in a standing-room-only area for about half an hour, and then we were sent out to retrieve our own bags. I walked out onto the tarmac and was amazed at what I saw. They had completely unloaded the baggage from the entire airplane. Bags were strewn halfway down the runway, and I had to find mine in this mess.

I had three bags and they were not in one place. I finally found them all and walked over to a baggage loader, and the man then checked my bags against my claim checks. Once he was satisfied, he loaded my bags onto the plane and allowed me to reboard. That process continued until every passenger was accounted for. After the airplane left the runway, it made a circle over the field, and I could see bags still sitting on the runway. If you missed your flight that day and your bags went ahead of you, you probably lost them on the runway at La Paz.

We touched down in Tijuana and I began to worry. The last stamp in my passport was from Costa Rica, and none from Mexico. I walked up to the clerk in the terminal, and she asked me for my passport. I handed it to her and expected the worst, but she said, "You were in Costa Rica, I see. I spend a lot of time there myself."

I didn't say a word about myself, but muttered, "That's nice." She stamped my passport and let me through the gate leading to transportation that would take me to the U.S.A. Border.

I boarded a van outside the terminal and headed for the safety of my homeland. We pulled up to the border and the lines were a mile long. I was in the front seat, and the driver told me to hold on tight. He swerved sharply to the left and entered a four-lane freeway off-ramp. He then continued — still heading the wrong way — onto the high-speed freeway, honking his horn like crazy at the oncoming cars which he dodged. He took the next exit, but that was actually an on-ramp. He continued to honk his horn wildly at more oncoming cars until he cleared the ramp. Then he swung the van sharply to the right and stopped at the first one of the border-crossing gates. He was at right angles to the gate and waited. When the car being served pulled forward, he pulled in front of the car that was supposed to be next.

The guard at this U.S. Customs gate saw him cheat to get in line, and walked over to the driver slowly, shaking his head, hopping mad, and said, "What's your story?" He didn't like the answer the driver gave him, so he ordered the driver to take the van over to the holding area, where we were all required to get out to be processed.

There were seven of us in the van, and the other six were very nervous. They were all Mexicans.

One of them was dressed in a N.Y. Yankees hat and T-shirt, and he was holding back a little. I decided to hold back also and let everyone else go ahead of me.

They opened every bag that belonged to everyone ahead of me in my line. Two of them started crying and were told that they could not pass — their papers were not in order. All of the people in the van were very brown, but they came by it naturally. I was also very brown from my suntan — resulting from being out at sea so long — and when the guard asked me where I was born, he was shocked when I told him Olympia, Washington.

I told him that I had been sailing, pulled off my sun glasses, and said, "See? Blue eyes!"

He laughed and said, "Get along with you, then," and passed me through. I got down on the U.S.A. ground, kissed it, and felt safe for the first time since I had left Panama. It had been a long and harrowing trip back to the States. I called my wife and told her where I was and noticed that the man in the N.Y. Yankee clothes was talking on the telephone next to me.

When we got back in the van, the driver called out our names and three passengers were missing. I explained to him about the two in front of me being sent back, and one of the other passengers had seen the man in the N.Y. Yankee clothes being picked up by another car. His exact words were, "Amigo vamoosed."

The driver laughed, and off we went. The van was a brand new van, and it was beautiful. It made the trip very comfortable, and now that I could see that he was driving on the proper side of the highway again, I was soon asleep.

I was awakened when the van abruptly stopped. We were out in the middle of nowhere at an old farmhouse. There were no houses in the immediate vicinity and my self-protection warnings started going off. I had heard of people coming across the border and being held for money by some of these transportation companies. I was just getting ready to run for it, when the driver said, "We change vans at this station, and I must go back to the airport in Tijuana. Thank you for your patronage." I looked around and there was an old van parked next to the farmhouse. It looked like it was on its last legs. The new driver waved to us, and the other people climbed into it. I was very apprehensive, but the other people in the van said that this was the normal way of doing things. The driver said that we were in San Ysidro,

California, motioned for me to get into the front seat, and off we went.

The driver headed back to the Interstate 5 Freeway, and we were being bounced badly on the rough road in the old van. It was quite a change from the other one, and I made sure that the driver knew it. I would have taken this old van to a wrecking yard.

We were south of Oceanside, Calif., when the traffic suddenly started to slow down. I looked ahead and the freeway was backed up for about a mile. The four lanes were being funneled down to two lanes, and there was a Border Patrol Guard in each lane checking cars. I noticed very tall — about 20-foot tall — chain link fencing on either side of the two lanes. That fencing formed a funnel to keep people from getting into the oncoming traffic or escaping by using the shoulder of the road.

We were in the right lane about ten cars from being checked through, when the people in one of the cars in the right lane opened its doors. It looked like eight to ten people jumped out and started running down the highway in the direction from which we had come and away from the Border Patrol. They were quickly chased down and subdued, and then the two lanes started moving again.

I instructed the driver to get into the left lane so that I could be the one to talk to the Border Patrol Guard. With my sunglasses off and in perfect English, I said, "Yes, we are all legal," and he waved us on through. The other people started clapping and thanked me for getting them passed through the check point. They were all legal, but like in Mexico, sometimes that was not always enough, and there could be sudden catches which might result in tragedy. The rest of the trip was quiet and peaceful, and I took local transportation from Los Angeles to Newport Beach where I would be staying with an old school mate of mine — Byron Chamberlain. I would be staying with him until I heard from the crew of the *El Jay*.

Byron owned Mariners Boat Insurance Brokerage Firm and also owned a large, older, wooden schooner named *The Rose of Sharon*. *The Rose* is about seventy-feet long and was built in the early 1930s. Byron had it anchored in Newport Harbor, and that would be my floating hotel until *El Jay* showed up in San Diego.

While I was there on the boat, my wife Judy flew down to join me. We were lucky enough to join Byron and his son Craig in the next schooner race off the California coast near San Diego. The race was a competition among old, wooden schooners, and they were all fast boats.

The wind was blowing about fifteen knots, and *The Rose of Sharon* responded on queue. We led the race most of the way, but we were eventually passed by a much larger schooner named *Kelpy*. Because of our handicap though, we still won the race on corrected time. It was a very exciting race and Judy and I had a blast. As I remember that day in 1986, Byron still held the record for wooden schooners sailing out of the Los Angeles area to Hawaii.

But on the way back to Newport Beach, we were intercepted by the U.S. Coast Guard. They were very curious about what we were doing offshore in the large boat, and stopped us to find out. That was the time of Ronald Reagan, and drug smuggling was going to be stopped if possible. Two officers boarded the boat with permission, and Byron explained about the race. They asked to check the boat's papers and our identification, and we complied. When they saw that everything was in order, we were happily on our way home again to Newport Beach Harbor. They were very polite and courteous — a stark contrast with the way I had been treated by some of the customs officers I had encountered in other countries on my recent journey in the *El Jay*. It was the first time I had been treated with respect on the whole trip.

Judy stayed for a week, enjoying the sunny days, and then reluctantly headed back to Olympia and the rain. That first week had passed by very quickly, but I was anxious for news from the *El Jay*. I figured that they would have arrived in Cabo San Lucas by now, and because they hadn't called me, I assumed they were headed north, which would put them in San Diego in about one week. They were to contact me immediately, and I would travel down to meet them at the moorage in San Diego.

It would be a long, second week, and the guilt of not being down there with them weighed heavily upon me. Finding myself in this position was very difficult. When there had been trouble, it always seemed that I had been the positive force that made a huge difference in the trip. Being out of the boat while they were still struggling was hard to live with.

My wife, over the phone, and Byron in person kept telling me to relax, that Bill was going to bring the *El Jay* to San Diego, and everything was going to be fine. The words rang hollow to me because of past problems, and I feared for the worst.

The second week went by, and then two more days, but I received no telephone call. I called my Lloyds of London Insurance Agent and asked him what to do. He assured me that two days would not be an abnormal delay because of the currents that flowed south along the west coast of California.

I telephoned Cabo San Lucas, and I was told that the boat had left nine days earlier. I then alerted the U.S. Coast Guard to be on the lookout for them, and they notified the Mexican authorities to be on the lookout as well. There was nothing left to do except wait.

After three weeks had passed, the insurance company was convinced that the boat had gone down. I asked them to give me some more time. I was left with the feeling that if I had been on board things would have been different.

After the fourth week, I was beside myself with grief. I was having to live with the possibility that three men were dead, and I had put them in that predicament. I called the insurance company and told them the bad news, and the agent was very sad for my loss. He said that he would start processing the paperwork for my claim for total financial loss of the boat and the three men on board.

I started to cry and had to excuse myself for a moment. He was very understanding and waited until I was composed. I decided that I was not ready to write off the *El Jay* and my three comrades yet, and that I would wait a little longer. I wanted to die myself.

Two days later, my telephone rang, and it was Bill's voice that I heard on the line. It was like a gift from Heaven. I could not answer him at first. Tears were flowing and I couldn't speak. And then I was afraid he would hang up before I could speak, thinking that there was no connection. I told him that I would be down to the moorage as fast as I could and headed for San Diego. If ever a prayer was answered, Bill's voice on the telephone was one.

I arrived at the moorage and found the three of them taking a well-deserved rest. Juan had fallen asleep holding onto a half-empty soda.

The boat was a complete mess. The engine had failed just one day north of Cabo San Lucas. They had decided to keep going under sail alone and were determined to make it to the U.S.A. Two days later, the roller-furling jib had severed at the top of the mast and fallen to the deck. They were left with no engine and no jib. The main and the small staysail were the only sails left to sail with.

They had to tack continuously to make any headway, and Bill told me that it took them two days to get by one small island. They would just get to the end of the island and the wind would die. The normal southerly current would carry them back to where they started from. The batteries had died because the engine was not running to charge them, and they traveled at night with flashlights hung from the mast. They were in the main shipping lanes, and that was their only method of signaling their presence to any ship traffic.

I didn't care about the boat because at that moment I was just glad to see them alive and well. I was informed by the U.S. Customs Officer at the moorage that Juan and Nouyo would be my responsibility. They would be allowed only a twenty-four-hour, temporary visa, and then they would have to leave the country. We all piled into my rented car and headed for lunch. They hadn't had a decent meal for four weeks.

After a large lunch, the two young men wanted to go shopping. We headed for the local stores. Juan purchased many different-sized fishhooks, and Nouyo purchased a water ski to take home to Istapa, Mexico. Bill, Juan, and I said goodbye to Nouyo, and then put him on a flight back to his home in Mexico. I wrote Bill a large check, and put him and Juan on their flight back home to Panama.

It was with a heavy heart that I watched each of them board the airplane. I felt good that they were all safe, but I was left with a feeling of sorrow. That would probably be the last time I would see any of them, and they had become like family. Some years later, however, I had been able find Nouyo on a trip I had taken to Istapa. He did not remember my name, but he did remember me quite well, and called out the name "El Jay" twice when he saw me. We had a very nice visit, and he was forty one at the time.

I called the insurance agent and told him the good news and the bad news. The good news was that the boat had arrived, but the bad news was that it wasn't going to be sailing anywhere in the near future in its present condition. The boat eventually had to be shipped to Olympia where it would undergo a complete rebuild. The engine was a rusted hulk, the fittings below the waterline were all pitted, and the roller furling would have to be replaced also. I had the boat loaded on a huge boat trailer and then flew home to Olympia. My dream trip was finally over. A trucking company from Washington would bring the El Jay home at last.

My boat was badly beaten and would need many months of repair, but I would bring the El Jay back to its original condition, and the boat would one day sail again. I placed the El Jay in the hands of a local boat builder, Sam Devlin, who was just getting started. He promised me he would do his best and he did, but that is a story for another time.

I am left with many mixed emotions from the experiences of the trip, but every individual must follow his or her dream to its end. I survived and over came all of the many obstacles that were thrust into my life. My two vastly different crews were blessings on the trip. The first crew could have left me with a bad engine and headed for home, but they stayed strong for me until the end. The second crew could have abandoned my boat when I wasn't onboard, but they stayed strong and did not let me down. I completed a difficult trip with my head held high and nobody got hurt or killed. If you have a yearning to sail around the world or try an individual, open-water passage, then my advise to you is to follow your dream. I have accomplished this trip and the memories will last forever. The fact that I have written my story is a testament to my determination to succeed no matter what the odds may be. When I started the trip, I had no open-water experience. After the trip, I am considered to be a world-class sailor. The *El Jay* will rise like the Phoenix and I will sail again. The reality of today is that my trip is finished, but I will always keep dreaming, because if there is one thing that I've learned in the seventy-two years of my life, it is that without the dreams of today, there will be no realities of tomorrow.

INDEX